Some Bo~

Clea Myers

LEAF BY LEAF

Published by Leaf by Leaf
an imprint of Cinnamon Press,
Office 49019, PO Box 15113, Birmingham B2 2NJ
www.cinnamonpress.com
The right of Clea Myers to be identified as author of this work has been
asserted by her in accordance with the Copyright, Designs and Patent Act,
1988. © 2024 Clea Myers.
Print Edition ISBN 978-1-78864-988-9
British Library Cataloguing in Publication Data. A CIP record for this
book can be obtained from the British Library.
Designed and typeset in Adobe Caslon Pro by Cinnamon Press.
Cover design by Adam Craig © Adam Craig
Cinnamon Press is represented by Inpress.

This book is a memoir. It reflects the author's personal memories and
opinions of experiences viewed with hindsight. To respect the privacy of
characters still living, names and characteristics have been changed, events
compressed, and dialogue recreated.

Acknowledgements

Sincere gratitude and thanks to Michael Jenkins, Diane Esguerra, Rowan Fortune, Jan Fortune and the team at Cinnamon Press.

About the Author

Clea Myers is an actress and writer who currently lives alone in Notting Hill. This memoir follows her cult bestseller, *Tweaking the Dream: A Crystal Meth True Story.*

For all of us still hoping and searching for our happy-ever-after, however that might manifest for you, dear reader. And for the boys who chose not to hear No; who abused and disrespected me, thank you. Without you I would not be the woman I am proud of today.

Nam Myoho Renge Kyo

Some Boys I Knew

Prologue

The romance you crave is now. You are the leading man or lady in this movie. Stop waiting on bouquets and start sending, stop dreaming of the grand gesture and make it. Drop everything and grab this chance to appreciate life's staggering beauty, starting with your own. Romance yourself 'til you become a love song and then serenade the world.

Rikki Beadle-Blair MBE, Reasons To Live

What the hell is wrong with me? Is it him? Me? Both of us? Why am I alone again?

I have pondered my relationship problems since I was first conscious of my dysfunctional patterns. It takes two to tangle, but must my tango always be so consistently off kilter? Haven't I put in enough rehearsal?

At forty-five, my thereabouts middle age, I took a break from men. I recognised something was wrong and needed to work out what. There had been too many disasters to think it was simply a case of choosing the wrong uns. I took myself back to investigate and perhaps unravel where I had erred.

A quality I have is a childlike naivety that is useful as an actress, but in every day life, not so much! I had hoped and believed that upon birth, and then publication of *Tweaking the Dream* my life would naturally become the stuff of dreams! But mucky life interfered. My first book,

T*weaking the Dream*, was the tale of my misguided move to Los Angeles in my early 20s, and forays into the film industry alongside a burgeoning, catastrophic addiction to crystal meth. (The dangerous street drug not yet part of mainstream consciousness through TV like *Breaking Bad*.) My time in LA had started well with a script development job at Propaganda Films, but my exploratory and adventurous nature alongside failures and disappointments led me down the wrong path. I spiralled into a life of tweaking, dumpster-diving and paranoia; in less than 2 years I'd spectacularly destroyed my American dream. A final trip to Sybil Brand County Jail saw me offered deportation back to the UK; I'd been living in the US on an H1 Visa (a specialty work visa allowing foreigners to work in the US), or spending at least 18 months in prison. They don't mess around in LA. Zero tolerance!

There was no doubt in my slurried mind jail would have been the end of me: metaphorically, physically, and spiritually. The two weeks I had already served was worse than anything I had experienced; granted I was coming down off meth, underweight, undernourished, and verging on insane, but anything—and I mean anything—was better than doing the time.

The intelligent part of me, hidden, whispered it would be the nail in an already damaged soul. Fatefully, my unwanted alien status played out in my favour and California washed their hands of me. My H1 Visa had been up for renewal, and naturally fallen off my list of priorities. Tragic, considering the hoops I'd jumped to get it in 1993.

(As a side note I found it ironic to discover recently

that Sybil Brand Country Jail was closed in 1997 and ever since been used in movies and television shows. So wonderfully Lala…)

While I wrote *Tweaking the Dream*, I wrongly hoped that once it was 'out there' I would somehow be magically cured and happy, cathartically cleansed. After all, my problem was drug addiction. That's what I'd been told over and over, along with the vague mention of 'abandonment' issues. And I had got off drugs, cleaned up and moved on, right?

In truth, life felt worse. I went into an early menopause due to Premature Ovarian Failure at thirty-seven, precipitating ME or chronic fatigue syndrome. Daily life became untenable, with little happiness. There were severe mood problems, joint pains, depression and a despair connected to the reality I'd never bear a child. Foolishly I'd hoped and believed that as a late developer, this would happen. Nowadays the menopause has become relatively accepted and discussed within the mainstream, but no one was speaking much about it in 2007/8. At least that was how I experienced it. My relationship with my mother fell apart again, in part due to mum's fury that I would now not give her any grandchildren. She'd never expressed any desire, but she was fed up with having to hear 'long-winded, boring stories from all my friends about their bloody wonderful, adorable grandchildren!' Again shame permeated. All I could do was bury it and try to keep going. Clearly, I had not upheld the unspoken obligation that a daughter provide her mother and father with at least one grandchild. A sense of isolation came into play. I embraced more self-care and integrative health measures to maintain what I now perceived as my damaged body.

A good friend and book editor said to me on publication of my first book: 'You really only scrape the surface about your relationships with men; it's like you are too scared to go there.' Her words set off my churning mind.

What do you mean, 'scared to go there?' I'd just exposed my drug-addled soul, and my questionable moral compass; what more can I do? But her words irked. Because my relationships, or lack thereof, might hold a key to my lifetime of mistakes.

Or more plainly, what the hell is wrong with me? Do I really, truly believe there is something wrong, or am I just re-enacting a hand-me-down story? A transgenerational tale of women behaving badly…

When I was a teenager, my mother had revelled in announcing how fickle I was, to all and sundry, when it came to boys and at the same time, telling me brazenly: 'Off with the old, and on with the new!' She claimed I'd be one of 'those women' who gets divorced 6 times. She would often regale me with the tale of her first marriage to my father in New York city. It was a glamorous wedding with Scottish bagpipers serenading the happy couple, and a fancy reception at the Carlisle Hotel. But all my mother recalled was the moment her mother—my grannie—drunkenly chased their going-away limousine. Grannie kept yelling: 'I hate you Bill Myers, I hate you.' A cousin had to grab and quickly escort her away before more damage was done, but my mother would redden in recounting this humiliation to me 20 years later. Mummy admitted to me she had married my dad at age 20 to get away from her own mother. She vaguely liked my father, but was not in love with him; he was her way-out; he was 40 and almost a confirmed bachelor. They'd met in the English countryside, in the village of Furneux Pelham in Hertfordshire when mummy had been staying with her guardian Molly, and my father was visiting his great uncle and aunt who'd looked after him during some of his school holidays from Winchester. Dad could hardly travel to and from Shanghai in China where his father worked as the last High Commissioner for Customs, married to his White Russian wife, a highly creative and emotional woman from what I have gleaned.

Mum was good at ruining significant events for myself—birthdays, college graduation—but I never gave her a wedding to destroy. Maybe she would have behaved with the utmost dignity and respect, but I will never know as she is no longer with us, and I'm certainly never getting married. To my mind, there is no point if children are not involved.

I believe transgenerational trauma is at play here. Transgenerational trauma is the psychological and physiological effects that the trauma experienced by people has on subsequent generations. The primary modes of transmission are the uterine environment during pregnancy causing epigenetic changes in the developing embryo and the shared family environment of the infant causing psychological, behavioural and social changes in the individual.

My grannie had also married a older man, a successful rubber-planter out in Malaya; she was 32, but she lied about her age because she would have been considered a spinster. Grannie had experienced a failed love affair with a fellow colonialist who promised to leave his wife for her, but never did. This affair, not her only one, precipitated my grandparents bitter divorce. My cuckolded grandfather was hellbent on revenge, spreading rumours that my grannie was a high-class call-girl and financially cutting off her and his only child, my mum. Grannie became extremely alcoholic, on top of her rather narcissistic traits. Fortunately, she was clever so she'd held down executive positions for a while in NYC, where she moved with my mother at age 12 who was unceremoniously taken away mid-term from her Sussex boarding school because her father now refused to foot the fees. But Grannie's pattern was to find a good job, only to mess it up months later through her alcoholic binges that saw her general behaviour deteriorate. My mum was spending many nights in Grand Central station to escape her mother's insanity at home. Grannie always promised my mum that she would be rich when her father died; his rubber plantation estate was worth well over a million pounds in 1972.

However, he chose a nephew who worked besides him, to receive the fruits of his labour overseas, leaving my mother a paltry £10,000 which she purchased a Tiger-skin coat and a white convertible MG. I think my mother was devastated at the contents of her father's will; why should the sins of the mother be passed onto the daughter who had done no impropriety? My mother attempted to mount a legal battle to challenge her father's will, which she called 'Operation Eagle', in her dramatic style. It was too costly to pursue, and my passive father was never one to enter a battle, not even under duress. My mother was materially fortunate; she still inherited no small amount from Molly, but that never seemed to salve or resolve her bitterness towards her father and his actions. It was like she was on a constant drip of perceived abandonment. She would later disinherit me when I displeased her one-too-many times.

I became a Nichiren Buddhist in 2001, and the daily practice of chanting the mantra Nam Myoho Renge Kyo expanded my life. Creating a sacred space in a corner of a room to sit and chant, holding a daily ceremony to celebrate my life and others, was a powerful daily tool. It elevated me—from a generalised low mood to one brimming with hope and potential; it also helped reframe my perception of others to a more compassionate point of view, and thereby myself. In this form of Mahayana Buddhism, the practice of chanting is seen as polishing a tarnished mirror; as humans all of us have this tarnish on our individual mirrors, or karma—from our upbringings, experiences, traumas, choices, social conditioning—but the chanting of Nam Myoho Renge Kyo polishes, or cleanses these impurities, enabling us to vibrate on a more loving, open, and connected field.

The other area that defeated me was my relationship with my mother. In this form of Buddhism, one is taught that all things are open to transformation. The idea thrilled me, but I continued to grapple with my complex and difficult mother. I'd make progress, but then the abuse would restart, a record scratching on repeat.

Around 2011, I was having therapy with an NHS psychologist at the Jordon Hospital and the idea that my mother was suffering with a personality disorder, specifically Narcissistic Personality Disorder (NPD), came into question. I read more about narcissism and felt convinced that my mother was an alcoholic narcissist. And that her mother was also one, and perhaps it went back further. My mother refused to ever take up therapy throughout her life, because she perceived it as 'typically American'—a bad thing in her eyes—and as she would often opine: 'I'm not the one with the problem here!' My outward search for inward answers—through spirituality and talk therapy—were seen as signs of weakness. She had done her best to make me strong, but I was a disappointing weakling. Except in one area: she never saw me cry. In fact, I did not properly cry from age 9 up to age 45. Quite an achievement in my estimation. She'd instructed me: 'Don't cry! It's too upsetting for me,' upon depositing me at prep school; like a good girl, I followed her orders to the letter.

As a teenager during school holidays, my ears had become tuned to hearing my mother and stepfather discuss me through the thick walls of their Warwickshire cottage. A typical exchange went like this:

'Why doesn't Clea have a boyfriend? All her friends do.'

'I have no idea.' My stepfather replied vaguely, adding as an afterthought, 'She's a bit on the wrong side of odd. I can only assume she takes after her pathetic father.'

'There's definitely something wrong with her. And she's going through a very plain stage.'

'She's certainly looking a little—'

'Fat!' Mum exclaimed.

'I was going to say podgy, but to be fair she has been sitting round studying a lot recently.'

'Well, I don't like it. It makes me look bad having a

fattie for a daughter. Grannie would have put me straight back on the Epsom salts. Quite frankly, she's an embarrassment.'

Their assumption that there was always something 'not quite right' or 'just plain wrong' about me, I now understand, were projections of their lack of self-worth; however, the criticisms, put-downs, and mercurial attitudes left an indelible mark. Can I 'erase' this by delving into recollections of these relationships? My answer: I don't know, but I must try.

What has become clear as I've dug into the wealth of my memory bank is that I had a straightforward agenda at certain times, usually wanting to fix a broken man. And a broken man can arrive in many guises.

I was determined, particularly in my 20s, to keep retesting the 'can't change men' theory as if my existence depended on it and then when I failed again, I internalised the blame and lost even more of the sense of who I was, what I valued and my own self-esteem. That I did not abide by defined standards is also clear; I was a brilliant overlooker. I could overlook bad or unacceptable behaviour if I believed myself 'in love', as if the feeling's intensity admonished all sins. Men stole from me, cheated on me, hit me, insulted, and abused me, but if I still felt a kernel of love, I'd overlook it, because it wasn't *that* bad, was it?

Denial is a powerful drug and the endorphin release following negative behaviours—the apologies, 'it will never-ever-happen-again' promises, the hot make-up sex, the re-bonding through confessionals—was an adrenaline fix of the highest order.

And I knew about getting high because during some

of this time I was addicted to drugs too. You might as well just call me the eternal fixer, looking everywhere but within.

I have learned you can't fix people or make them change. No other person can do that for another. All these years, I'd been looking for validation from broken men. And the couple I dated who were not broken, I reversed roles and did my best to break them with my bad behaviour. I'd given my power away, repeatedly, and some part within me felt justified causing these men suffering; a horrible, low-minded tit for tat.

In this memoir I have revisited all my past relationships—any of significance however short the liaison—to see what happened, in the hope of working out my destructive patterns. I have tried to be fair, looking at both our limitations, character flaws, expectations, addictions, and anything else relevant. It has been an uncomfortable and revealing journey for me, but dear Reader I hope an interesting one for you.

That I treated myself so poorly for most of my dating years makes me unequivocally sad, but I now have my own evidence on paper. There are no more excuses I can tell myself!

Although many of these destructive patterns are hardwired, I am actively transforming them, through healing practices and therapy, and starting to have respectful, nurturing, loving relationships. Inner transformation is possible. I determine to be the change I want to feel internally and see externally. And love is not the reserve of the young, but an option open to us all, if we choose to open our hearts fully with the courage and wisdom of the knowledge gained from the lessons life has given us.

Naturally our parents provide the template for our relationships, with ourselves and others. Mine separated when I was six because my mother fell madly in love with another man. Without 'falling madly in love' from time to time, my mother reckoned life not worth living. After a two-year affair following my birth, she left my father, who was devastated, and we shortly moved to Ottawa, Canada to be by her lover's side where an oil company had posted him.

I always knew he saw me as a necessary evil; he'd never wanted children, but I came with my mother as a readymade package and he was just about willing to compromise. I was clearly instructed to be 'seen but not heard', as the Victorian saying goes. I think part of him realised a wife and a cute, blonde six-year-old was good for his company-man image.

For me, I was appalled by his unsavoury habit of strutting naked at home: witnessing his hideous, hanging appendage. My disgust fuelled their laughs in what I would later know to be a form of triangulation. He also liked to play grownups with me by slipping his tongue in my mouth whenever he managed to get near enough to kiss me on the lips. His behaviour was inappropriate, but he wasn't a child molester: mummy and him liked to use me for laughs. Whether it was my repelled response to him trying to kiss me, or ridiculing my ballet shows (I was left-footed), at least I received attention.

Mummy also liked to retell me the lie that my father was insistent about me attending boarding school in England. We were 8 hours away by plane so the thought of this sent me into tearful bouts, which then prompted my mother to comfort me with the words: 'I will not let that happen to my baby girl!' Her words were false; 3 years later off I went to prep school in Berkshire. By that point mum had persuaded her husband to leave his career-making position in Ottawa, and return to their farmhouse near Bishops Stortford. Her timing was rather off as the UK entered a recession in 1977; he could not find any kind of job, let alone with his beloved BP. The vaguely varnished blame ran deep within him, and manifested in her 'suicide' attempts. I spent hours hiding in the disused henhouse, in a spinney at the top of the garden whenever I was back with them on school holidays. I split the time with them and my father so in some ways you could say I was lucky.

My actual father, a product of World War Two, public school and Oxford, was older than all my friends' dads because he'd not married till forty. To me his demeanour shouted 'don't touch me!' In truth, I know that his era just didn't value touch and the untold grief he suffered as a young man, losing his three best friends from Winchester to the war, is beyond my personal experience. On the flipside of my shy, withholding dad, who I really did not see often anyways, I had pushy, flashy stepdad who made my skin crawl.

Freud asserted: *'Women think they marry their fathers, they don't, they marry their mothers.'*

My relationship with my mother has proven the trickiest of my life. I believe her to be an alcoholic narcissist; I have researched the subject relentlessly. If I put her on the spot she had no problem lying: at age 7 I'd rushed home from school in Ottawa in floods of tears.

'What's wrong?' she demanded.

'Is it true, is it true?'

'Is what true, sweetie?'

'That the man puts his thing inside the woman's tummy through her pee-pee parts, to make a baby?'

A lengthy pause followed; her glance averted to the river across the road.

'Who told you that?'

'Tom and Jimmy in gym class. And Sonia says everyone knows it's true.'

'Of course it's not true. What a silly thing to say!'

She then found some Reese's peanut-butter cakes in the cupboard and sent me off to my room with a plateful.

Maternal feelings were never prominent, and she forgot to tell me about the onset of puberty and menstruation. When I witnessed spotting in my knickers age eleven, I thought I was close to death. Matters were not helped when she sent my stepfather out to the shops to buy sanitary towels. That he should hold such intimate knowledge about me was a bitter pill worsened by his remarks about me 'becoming a woman.'

The fact of bleeding, and on a monthly basis, disgusted me. As we all know, clarity arrives with hindsight, but I can equivocally state that this transition from girl into woman was laced with a fear and latent shame I did not then comprehend. That my mother's transition had been awkward as well was proven years later when she explained her story: She had got her period young at the boarding school she attended in Sussex because her parents lived in Malaya, where her elderly father was a rubber planter in Serenbem. Her mother, my grannie, wreaked havoc with her married lover who never left his wife, and soon after that disappointment, her life became defined by alcoholism.

My mother felt her time living in a tropical climate had resulted in her earlier-than-normal development. Such was her fear and shame she had used cut rags in secret to staunch the flow of blood, and afterwards hid them under her bed in a big, old brown leather suitcase. On conducting an inspection of her dormitory, the school matron came on this small trunk, flinging it open: the rancid, iron smell made her gag. Further shame and humiliation meted out on a young girl—undoubtedly feeling abandoned and alone—thousands of miles from home.

Even when my mother told me this story, when she was well into her 60s, I knew I was the first and last person she shared it with. That a young girl could feel so scared in an institution expensively caring for her is appalling, but not unusual in the British boarding school tradition. I was sent to boarding school myself at age nine. Sadly no one prepared her, and she carried the baton, unwittingly. My mother was never one for self-reflection. For me, the onset of puberty and menstruation was riddled with angst; however, it quickly settled in the all-female boarding-school environment where we laughed and joked about 'Rufus' like it was a minor nuisance. When you are young and growing, what feels likes a life-changing catastrophe morphs into something verging on mundane. But then so many things are going on, it's exciting and overwhelming all at once. At the time I don't think I gave these changes much thought, beyond the initial, elemental fear experienced on the sight of blood from a private orifice. Still, my relationship with womanhood and potential motherhood proved my greatest wound.

I don't blame my parents, but I recognise the roles they played in the drama that resulted in my defection from the life of coupledom, and marriage.

From a young age I had faith. Maybe it was the enforced chapel attendance at school, but deep down I believed that things, or life, worked out for the best—the universe supported me. In my teens my mother went through a nasty divorce from flash stepdad, and ended in the hospital having tried to take her life. Afterwards, I remember sitting in her Edwardian four poster bed with her at her farmhouse in Hertfordshire, dunking Ginger Nuts in my morning tea before she collapsed into tears. I felt possessed as I promised her things would get better and she just had to believe it.

She always remembered that exchange.

In another strangely lucid but drunker moment, she claimed it helped her to carry on. She reconciled with my stepfather; things did improve for her, but her treatment of me did not. Narcissistic Personality Disorder often results in a high level of oftentimes secret abuse to close family members, and in our case, it was namely myself that received the brunt of it, although her husband was sometimes in the firing line too.

Chapter 1

First Love: Luke

Whatever our souls are made of, his and mine are the same.

Emily Bronte, Wuthering Heights

Regarding Luke, my first love, I was blessed in one way: I lost my virginity with him, and it was tender, romantic, and loving. Most of my boarding school friends suffered an undignified fumble and penetration behind the lacrosse pavilion, or late at night on the drawing room sofa at a house party. My introduction to the delights of love-making was perfect. This initial 'triumph' in the relationship stakes made me feel that little bit special. More fool me…

My teenage years of the 1980s were filled with balls. Not balls as in testicular, an area I had zero experience of, but as in fancy, 'dress-up' parties. 'Unbridled lust among upper-class Lolitas and public-school Lotharios', exclaimed *The Sunday Telegraph*. We'd be gussied up in over-priced strapless taffeta creations—Sasha Hetherington's tiny shop on Kings Road was my personal favourite; prancing like banshees to 80s hits while glugging muscadet, and snogging our male equivalents in black tie. The decade was awash with these parties—

ornery or fruity sounding gallivants like the Feathers, Blossom, Bluebird, Blizzard—and I was desperate to be seen at them all. Like any self-respecting Sloane I was desperate to get everything right and fit in, wearing too much turquoise eye-shadow and speaking loudly in self-important, plummy tones.

Luke and I met at the Bluebird Ball held at Heaven Under the Arches in London's West End, a glorified disco in a metropolitan village hall. I was fifteen and he was seventeen. He held a combined resemblance to the actor Brad Pitt and the hapless character Lofty from *EastEnders*.

Luke side bumped me as I stood at the edge of the dance-floor watching in horror as my tortoiseshell antique hair-comb, recently fallen off my head, was carelessly kicked about. That afternoon I'd made a floppy black velvet bow to sew on the comb and I was pleased with how it had come out. 'If you lose that you'll be in trouble!' My mother's snappy warning echoed.

Before I'd said anything to him, Luke swooped into the melee and retrieved the antique comb, strutting on and off the dance floor like a peacock. I took this as a sign he was to be my latter-day knight. I felt myself going red. I wasn't good at openers, or banter. But clearly, he'd noticed me before the comb had fallen out.

'There you go!'

'Thanks.'

'At least now it won't die from the bashings of some flat-footed oaf to the death knell of *Come on Eileen*.'

Did I mention he was funny?

I clocked his wispy blond hair loosely touching the deliberately undone thread of his black silk bow-tie.

'Don't you remember me?' he asked.

'Should I?' A beat. I felt cool in that moment.

'We met at Eton… When you came to visit Amanda's brother. I'm in the same house as him. I played you some Supertramp because you'd never heard the Airplane song. Remember?'

'Oh yes! You were the one that had really cool things on your walls!'

'Things? My flags you mean; Che Guevara, courtesy of Athena.' I remembered how I had been struck by the flowing fabrics pinned about his room, giving it a Bedouin tent feel. I had assumed boys didn't go in for that sort of thing. I had not paid Luke much attention as I was more interested in someone else that afternoon.

Back at the dance-floor, we'd reached an awkward impasse as to what to say or do next, when a glamorous brunette with an up-do swept up beside him with exuberant air kisses. None for me, I noticed, although I had met her quite a few times; par for the course in such circles. She then slid her arm through Luke's and shoved him in the direction of her friend who 'was dying to meet him'. He looked back over his shoulder at me as he was led away, mouthing 'I'll be back'. I was miffed, but I had a feeling this was the beginning.

At school I received a letter from him. Because we were both at boarding school this meant things got to simmer, while many pages of light blue Basildon Bond got scrawled over, screwed up and written, and sent to Windsor from my school, Heathfield, all of twelve miles away in Ascot. Letters were exchanged—one was signed '*te quiero*' (I want/love you) and I went into conniptions of delight. Plans were hatched: The big plan was the inter-railing trip throughout Europe for a month in the summer. I had just finished my O levels, Luke his As and I somehow managed to convince my parents that going round Europe by train for a month was normal for a sixteen-year-old girl. In the 80s this would have been considered laissez-faire parenting, just as unplanned pregnancy and subsequent abortion was considered shameful.

I believed my heart would break if I wasn't allowed to go. Having divorced parents supported my cause: my mother was too self-involved to care, and my sweet dad too introverted to express what he felt. I'd craftily learned to play them off each other and my mother was already emotionally overwhelmed. The 'love of her life', my stepdad, had kicked her out of the marital home in Dubai, where he'd been posted for work a few years ago. They were in the middle of a messy divorce and my absence gave her licence to fall apart and blame someone else.

Luke made the trip seem more supervised with some parental involvement. We started in Geneva. Simon, his best friend also at Eton, had parents that lived on the Lake and we were to spend ten days with them. There were six of us—three boys and three girls, of which I was the youngest by two years.

Bizarrely I recall finding a New York City cop wallet in a cupboard at my dad's house and decided this tooled, black leather object would prove a good conversation opener with the older girls, whom I had never met. One of my best friends from school helped me carry my bags on the tube to Waterloo. I was nervous. Once on the train I ceremoniously brought out this wallet and showed it to Emily and Davina. It was just a black wallet. They both smiled politely and changed the subject to Emily's shoes, fabulous gladiator style sandals, as I cringed in the corner and Luke looked away, embarrassed for me.

I'd had little experience mixing socially with boys, except at county parties and charity balls, so spending extended down time, hour on hour on trains and buses, was uneasy; banter was not part of my repertoire. They all played cards, something I avoided, so I'd sit in the corner and try to read, trying not to feel completely left out.

The point of this inter-railing trip was to spend time with Luke, and luckily most of the time he was equally keen. We were usually wrapped in each other like hungry snakes and it was divine. I felt grown up and couldn't wait to get up into the Swiss Alps where we were headed after Lake Geneva; where we could be properly alone together. Sexual tension was on the verge of eruption. I was sharing a room with Emily and the boys were down in the games room in the basement. Late one night, Luke and I almost went 'all the way' ensconced on a maroon velvet sofa in Simon's parents' drawing room, but I kept pushing him off in rhythm to every creaky sound in the house. I couldn't bear the shame of getting caught with my pants down, so-to-speak, although Luke wasn't at all concerned.

This trip was full of firsts: first proper boyfriend, first holiday alone with said boyfriend, and losing my virginity. After our civilised stay on Lake Geneva, we all took a train up into the Alps. Finally, Luke and I were in a room by ourselves, in a local pensione and were free to do as we chose. The build-up was excruciating and I had driven the girls mad with my sexual neuroses.

At last, to the tinny sound of one of Luke's mixed tapes, full of Supertramp, Dire Straits and Stevie Wonder, this sensitive young man and I came together. He was gentle and we were in love; it was magical, with only a tiny momentary discomfort. It was a great introduction to love and sex and I felt blessed. I'd heard predominantly horror stories from my female circles that would now be considered 'rapey', or perfunctory. Luke was my knight. I was a willing victim to the Patriarchy, as my mother had been, but I did not understand this then.

Undeniably, Luke and I were besotted. We discussed plans like me leaving restrictive Heathfield and taking my A levels at Kirby Lodge, a girls' sixth form college near Cambridge, while he interned at Kleinwort Benson in the city, and travelled the USA. And fitting in his beloved skiing in Verbier, where incidentally he wanted to get married. His obsession with Verbier made me uneasy.

Luke was a ski fanatic and part of his gap year was to be spent as a ski bum in Verbier before taking his place at Cambridge.

Teenage hormones were the glue holding us together, a potent force that felt like true love. I don't think I have ever felt so physically passionate about anyone, a magnetic experience. And it was reciprocal, initially. Our closeness felt special.

Spring in Verbier and I was back in the Swiss Alps to meet with Luke on a skiing holiday. Being a teenager, I didn't understand how a mere six months can alter your persona. Or so it seemed with Luke. When I met him, he had been confident, but not arrogant. If I had known what lay ahead, I would have left my Moonboots down in Dad's cellar. The trip was organised by Simon, known to me from the inter-railing trip, and there were eight of us booked in to a pensione in town. I shared a room with

Emily, also from the inter-railing trip. She ended up going out with Luke, after she lost half her body weight on a vegetable-only diet. I'd never thought she was in the least overweight, but it seems the snide comments from boys, while we swam, boated, and sunbathed on Lake Geneva, hit their mark. I had zero body issues then.

Luke had already been bumming out in Verbier a couple months. Growing up, Luke's father was a diplomat in Switzerland so he had skied constantly in childhood. He was looking particularly handsome, tanned skin and long blond hair past his collar, the boyishness gone and replaced with the youthful exuberance of a young man setting off on a charmed life. When I caught sight of him, through the glass of the hotel lobby, after months apart, I felt vaguely winded at just how good looking he was. From that moment I never quite believed he could see me as an equal. Perhaps I subconsciously detected what would become evident? Our sexual energy remained; we found ourselves upstairs in the single pensione bed pronto, but I immediately felt his need to be elsewhere, like he was always vaguely distracted.

I was not an experienced skier, but I could perform the basic motions at a relaxed pace. I had learned cross country as a child in Ottawa where I lived a couple years with my mother and stepfather, and then I'd been to Courcheval on a school trip. Luke was an expert and within an hour became irritated and impatient. It was like I was letting his image down, being unable to coast the steepest moguls I'd ever seen. After our first afternoon on the slopes, I was reduced to tears, a shivering wreck slumped at the side of the mountain. He skied off, shaking his head. I was whiney, but he acted bad on purpose.

Saying stuff like; 'Oh my god! You are just so pathetic!' and harrumphing while waiting for me to catch up, checking out the stream of pretty girls that bobbed by.

Luke had warned me before he couldn't spend all his time with me. He'd made a load of new friends he was not overly keen to introduce me to; he was staying in a chalet that again he claimed was a long way out of the main village, and there was not enough room for me. In the mornings, around 9am, he snuck into the hotel and up to my room where he sidled up to me in bed, eager for morning sex. I took all this in my stride, trying to maintain my cool in the face of many other young Sloanes, all of whom Luke knew. Any café, bar, or restaurant we entered was full of braying chit-chatty people familiar with him. I noticed he always introduced me as 'Clea', not 'Clea, my girlfriend' when he remembered his manners and introduced me at all; often I would stand mutely until someone acknowledged me. I felt out of my depth and he was not helping; Verbier was his lair and somehow it felt like I had landed there by accident; he could tolerate me, but not embrace my presence.

I had one ace: one of the other boys with us, Phil, had taken a shine to me. Another Etonian a year below Luke, Phil had a cute, rounded, and friendly face. Harry was his sidekick—pale, dark, and thin—with moody good looks. I got on well with Harry as we shared a love for surrealist cinema. We'd joked about ditching the skiing for the day and taking off to see a film, something no one else understood because they all held skiing sacrosanct. Now I understand these people are not my tribe, but I didn't know that then; I was desperate to fit in.

Luke came and went from our hotel as it suited and I skied, ate and drank with the others, pretending I was okay with the status quo, and that I was mature and grown-up.

No one wants to be seen as a cling-on so I kept my head down. A few evenings in and I was drinking on the hotel room's balcony with Harry and Phil. We tended to 'front-load' before hitting a nightclub because drinks out were prohibitively expensive. I had a couple of light beers while the boys ploughed through some whiskey, more determined to get pissed. I looked at my watch and noticed it was past ten; Luke usually showed up around 8pm, after we'd all finished our dinner in the hotel restaurant.

'I wonder where Luke's got to? I'm sure he said he'd be here by now.' I swigged my warm beer while admiring the beautifully lit village against the bright white snow, when I noticed a subtle but knowing look pass between the boys. Their drunkenness was catching them off-guard.

'What? What's going on?' A sinking feeling invaded my stomach. Phil quickly looked away, mumbled 'nothing', while Harry was at a loss. No one said anything for what felt like minutes; the only noise was Emily's hairdryer from inside the room.

'What do you know about Luke? Come on, you're supposed to be my friends!' I appealed to their better natures. Phil was reticent and poured himself more whiskey, his get-out clause. This almost tipped me over the edge as their denial infuriated me.

Harry, with a sharp intake of breath, raised both his arms in surrender. 'Fuck it! Clea, you need to know what's been going on behind your back.'

'Hellooo! Can someone please show me decency here?' I intuited I was about to be smashed in the gut.

'Luke has another girlfriend. And he's having dinner with her and her family right now.' Harry almost whispered.

'What? No. No way...'

An awkward silence followed.

'Another girlfriend? How does that work in this situation? Who is she? Come on, you're totally taking the piss.'

'I wish I was, sweetheart. I can tell you right now, I think his behaviour is despicable. Treating you like this.'

Phil nodded, although I noticed he hadn't added anything else despite being equally appraised. School honour no doubt, covering for the cool guy above him.

'You still haven't answered my question: who the hell is she, this conniving bitch?'

'...Poppy, that's her name. And she's here with her family—her parents, a sister and brother—in their chalet. They own a place. They've been here weeks and he's staying with them.'

I knew Luke had a need to feel part of a family, on account of his rather austere experience of family life. Yes, already I was finding excuses for him. Then anger, hurt and disbelief took me over. I grabbed the whiskey off the glass table and swung a couple of mouthfulls, spluttering and coughing at its sharp burn.

'Does everyone know? I mean all of you, Simon, Emily, everyone else?'

'Emily doesn't.' Phil added as if that would be a huge consolation.

'But all you boys know. And he's been traipsing to and

from here to there, keeping us both on ice? I don't believe it!'

'I think he told Poppy he'd broken up with you. She's actually really nice.' Andy added, embarrassed by his admission. I wanted to hit him.

'I'm sure she's delightful, I can't fucking wait to meet her.' Harry gave me a sympathetic look and draped his arms around my shoulders. I wanted to cry, but the tears wouldn't come. I buried my head in his shoulder.

'Thank you for telling me. For having the basic decency, unlike some other people.' I glanced pointedly at Phil who shrugged, mouthing sorry. Emily poked her perfectly coiffed head round the balcony door.

'Hiya! Why the sullen faces? What's going on? Luke's on his way up, he just called from Reception.' We all looked at each other uncertainly.

'Everyone just get out now. Please!'

'Okay. Okay yah. Don't take it out on us. We're your friends, remember?' Harry reminded me.

Confused, Emily looked at me questioningly. 'Clea, what's happened?'

The boys nudged her back into the hotel room and I heard her rustle into her ski jacket; the door slammed behind them; soon after there was a quick sharp knock. I had quickly reapplied my glossy, frosted pink lipstick and re-teased my long high-lighted blonde hair that bounces over my forehead and flicks over on one side, like every other public school girl.

He stood there looking forlorn and a smidge guilty. He knew I knew, having passed the others on their way out. This irked me as if everyone was having a jolly good laugh behind my back, thinking what a little fool for love I was.

What an idiot I am. And, horror of all horrors, following in my mother's footsteps, a total 'fool for love'.

I took a deep breath; I hated confrontation and had never been in a similar situation. I wondered how my mother would handle it and had to stop myself from lapsing into a hysterical state. Determined to prove that I am a grown-up woman who knows how to deal with difficult things, like errant men, I wanted to believe that like any decent guy, Luke would be sorry. That he would want to make it up to me because after all I was his perfect half to make a whole. He stood in the doorway looking nonchalant and slightly pissed off with everything. And very sexy in faded jeans, mussed blond hair and a red checked shirt. His style had improved since he left school. His cute dorkyness gone.

'Are you coming in, or what?' I attempted to hide the angry edge in my tone.

'Yeah, sure sweetie, got a beer?' He had never ever called me sweetie so pointedly and I was not liking the way it sounded in his plummy, low tone. It felt reptilian. I grabbed a bottle of beer out of the mini-fridge and thrust it at him so it almost slipped out of his long-fingered hands.

'Steady there, sweetie!'

'Stop calling me fucking sweetie, will you?'

A long pause. 'What's wrong, Clea?'

'What the hell is going on? I can't believe you! Who is this girl you're two-timing me with? I'm disgusted— you've been going from my bed to hers and back. Ugh, I just feel sick!'

'Oh come on, Clea, it really wasn't like that. I mean me and her are just really good friends. And I know her family, they've been coming to Verbier forever and…' His voice trailed, leaving only a sharp tension. His closeness to the family hit a nerve. He was not close to his cold family and my family is no normal setup. I suspected we both secretly craved acceptance into a big, happy, normal family.

'And? And what? Where does that leave us?'

He looked at me with something like surprise. Was he still in with a chance to smooth things over? This is what I am praying for in my heart.

'Sorry sweet… I mean Clea, but I suppose we need to break up.'

'But I came out here on holiday especially for you! I changed so many things around to make this work out with my school holidays and my mum, and everything. I can't believe you are doing this to me.'

'Things happen. We had a good time, a great time actually. I do still love you, but…' He walked across the room and flung open the balcony door, letting in an icy draft. It felt like I had been kicked in the core, over and over—an inner emptiness made me gag for breath. That Luke was capable of this cruelty shocked me. I looked at him for a suggestion of comfort or kindness, a quality he'd seemed full of when we'd met. I wanted him to take me in his arms and make it okay again.

Behind him I put my arms tight round his waist.

He jerked me away. 'No please Clea, don't.' I couldn't quite believe that only that morning, all of twelve hours ago, we made love in that very room and now he flinched at my touch.

I went down on my knees. On my knees! I am on my knees, begging. I am seventeen years old and I think this is the worst thing that could happen to me. In that moment, that is how it felt. Luke was clearly uncomfortable, like he was picking up on my real pain and did not want to have to engage with it. He had not counted on me losing all dignity, because I appeared strong and proud. It was a first. Before this humiliating moment, I had felt so fortunate in the 'avoiding pain' stakes, having had such a great first love experience.

It had never crossed my mind he would cheat on me. Luke had been the most adoring and attentive boyfriend. On one of our first 'dates', although we never called them that, we'd stayed up all night talking about my difficult relationship with my mother. We sat at the kitchen table in a borrowed house on Highlever Road in West London, talking and kissing. Once the sun was up, I walked him to Latymer Road tube and he went to Paddington to get back to Eton, his absence undiscovered by his Housemaster. How the tables had turned; only a year ago he was in my shoes and not even aware of it. Perhaps I had more fickle moments than I'd like to admit.

The Christmas before my mother had booked a last-minute holiday for me and her to Porto de Mazarron in Spain. She'd visited a couple times before and started an on-off affair with the British tour operator, unbeknown to me. It was an off-beat place she'd discovered as balm during her separation from her husband. The night before I was due to leave for this holiday, Luke had stood on my door step, refusing to leave: we would part outside the house, hug and kiss, he would go to leave through the chipped maroon iron gate, walk a few paces, then swing back and approach me with open arms. The first couple times I stayed still and obliged, but then I went inside and shut the door. But he kept returning and knocking the brass knocker until I opened it and kissed him goodbye, again and again.

He did this three times. I had found it endearing, but then I obviously clocked his neediness—never attractive—and told him to go and not come back, because I still needed to pack. He'd also given me a large Christmas card covered in his trademark token of 'love': all the available white space covered in tiny crosses. I remembered how excited I had been the first time he'd given me a birthday card with the same tiny kisses all over it and marvelled at his commitment to this time-consuming detail. All this had led me to perceive Luke as rather a romantic soul, which did not fit with him seeing and sleeping with two girls at once. But I had then had a kiss with a handsome Spaniard on New Year's Eve, rather than calling Luke back in London as promised. My mother had called Luke instead, telling him I had food poisoning. It was a mother-daughter bonding moment, although she'd remind me of it when she felt I'd taken the moral high ground with her; an easy stance to take as she had so few morals. Fear of abandonment brings out a myriad of self-destructive behaviours.

Back in the Swiss hotel room I could see Luke's conscience catching up with him while I kept babbling about how good and right we were together, scared that if I'd let up an unsatisfactory denouement would occur. I thought he would relent: I moved closer and hugged his knees.

He exhaled a long sigh; then jerked out of my grasp towards the door, his mind made up. 'I'm really sorry, Clea. I never meant to hurt you.' His hand was on the door handle.

'I broke up with you, you bastard. I broke up with you!' I screamed at his back. The door closed quietly. I crumpled into a heap on the floor, great sobs stuck in my throat. My life over.

Emily found me crumpled up in a ball on the light brown carpet an hour later. I was worn out emotionally, but grateful to have a friend who'd not forgotten about me. We didn't know each other well, but she was kind and insisted the others from our ski group were waiting for me to join them in a bar. I looked a wreck, but she helped me fix myself up, lending me a fitted Kookai sweater that went with the grey-green of my bloodshot, panda eyes.

Unsurprisingly the cure-all for my boy trouble was alcohol and as soon as we arrived at the bar, the boys from our group plied me with drinks. If I'm honest I suppose I knew my grand love with Luke was not going to be finished in a ten-minute spat in a Swiss pensione. Hence, I started to milk and enjoy the drama. I think I liked being the centre of attention, at least for the evening. I knew that even if the boys didn't say it, they thought Luke's behaviour was shoddy and some were also jealous he'd managed to hook two pretty girls at once; I found out Poppy was pale-skinned, pixie-like and dark, the polar opposite to my tanned, streaky blondeness.

Around 1pm, when everyone sober enough to still stand remained, mainly on the glitter-balled dance-floor of the Farm Club, I glanced at Luke striding in, on a mission. He stood with a couple of cooler, older ski-bums markedly ignoring me. I took this opportunity to dance flirtatiously with Phil to *Whole of the Moon*, a song I'd always associated with Luke. A few bars before the track changed and Luke stalked over to me where he grabbed me from Phil; he whispered in my ear, 'I still really love you.' We were back in each other's arms to the sultry throes of *Careless Whisper*. The schmaltzy saxophone arrangement reached a crescendo with my roaring, drunken heart while the words about 'guilty feet have got no rhythm' were rather apt, as dancing was never Luke's forte. One of the few things he wasn't good at.

In a nutshell the innocence of first love could never be recaptured, but there were romantic moments I recall vividly to this day. Like when I got the day off school and jumped on the train to London to attend my mother's fiftieth birthday lunch at San Lorenzo's and afterwards, she tipsily waved £50 at me, telling me to take Luke to the Rivoli bar at The Ritz for champagne cocktails. I walked in and saw the side of his wispy blond Adonis head and tall, svelte figure in a pinstriped suit leaning against the bar. I thought how marvellous he was, but also how lucky I was that he was mine. He proposed off-the-cuff using a plain gold ring. I thought it was so grown up, but somehow unreal. I teetered back to Kirby Lodge late that evening, having dragged myself away from him to jump in a taxi and get the last train back to Cambridge. It did seem somehow perfect as Luke was coming up to Cambridge, to attend Clare College in months. It was part of our cunning plan. And then the plan fell apart. First love is like that I suppose.

I'd never had Luke down as spiteful, but after we did break up a few months following my trip to Verbier, he dated and slept with a wide range of our acquaintances. I believed this was to spite me, but he claimed it was hardly his fault as we shared and mixed within the same social pool, and in his words: 'You can't blame me if there's just so many hot girls we both happen to know!' Indeed.

As the next few years passed, we would meet from time to time; I'd say the sexual attraction was still there, but I was in no way in true contact with my feelings. I can't speak for him, but the worst part was when he dated one of my best friends from Heathfield. She also deceived me, insisting they were just 'great friends with the same sense of humour', but another friend confirmed their happy union while I was setting up my life in L.A., following my graduation from Brown university. This girlfriend was someone I had literally grown up with at boarding school—we'd shared everything from first periods to our initial sexual experiences to parental divorces, et al. That hurt.

From what I gather Luke is now a happily married, family man living the high life in New York. I did reach out on Facebook, for old times' sake really, but he was not forthcoming. He strikes me as a person who has skated through life, entitled and privileged, never having to suffer the consequences of his behaviour. However, that is purely my guesswork.

It could have been worse, right? No, wrong!

Chapter 2

The 151 Years

I do not wish for women to have power over men; but over themselves.

Mary Wollstonecraft, A Vindication of the Rights of Women

Hindsight is cruel; I know the turning point when everything went wrong; that 'crucial moment' in my life when things changed for the worse. An age-old, highly unoriginal problem: I got pregnant at age eighteen.

Back in the late 1980s respectable girls did not get pregnant in their teens, unless they were married. It was shameful, a confirmation that you were a slut. This was gender-based as young men were lauded for their virility, attractiveness, and popularity with us girls.

When I understood I was pregnant I experienced a meltdown. And the reality that it had happened via a two-night-stand compounded my self-hatred and shame.

It had started with an unrequited obsession with a guy; my response to his lack of interest was to reassign my affections to a friend of his I had not even met! I had, however, heard everything about him and credited him with all sorts of qualities, chiefly being good boyfriend material.

Timothy was enrolled at St Andrew's University and

one Friday during my year-off we piled into a friend's Audi and drove up there in record time, blaring Stevie Winwood. Timothy and I did hit it off, although I didn't find him attractive. It was the idea of him that attracted me, or perhaps the hope that the one I was obsessed with would hear about it. Timothy and I kissed late into the night to a soundtrack of the Beatles, *All You Need Is Love*. And then we left back for London having made vague plans to reconnect at Christmas in London. He hadn't called, but I ran into him at my regular hot spot, The 151 Club on Kings Road. (I'd been given a free membership by Adrian, one of the owners, at age seventeen.)

Timothy claimed he had called me, but I'd been out. I chose to believe him; my father did not have an answering machine yet. All I remember is waking in my friends' parents double-bed in Smith Street in Chelsea, a stone's throw from the night club. I had no recollection of having had sex with Timothy. There was no condom, or wrapper anywhere, so I took it that we had not had sex. I had been too drunk to remember and surely a decent young man like Timothy would not take advantage of a paralytically drunk girl? I recall another drunken encounter after much alcohol consumption at his place. Our brief hook-up was not memorable. We were both drunk and I would not have given it another thought if I had not got pregnant. We did meet again; he invited me to his flat, but he was also entertaining a group of Uni friends and barely gave me the time of day. I crept away feeling lost. Months later when the pregnancy showed up, there was no way I was speaking to him. He hadn't cared for me, so why would he care about this?

I had gawped at the nurse when she'd confirmed I was

pregnant. She looked perplexed and asked: 'Didn't I feel that anything was awry within my body?' I hadn't, after all, had a period for three months, but I had not given it much thought. One less thing to worry about.

I then went back to my father's house and hid under the duvet for 48 hours. I couldn't eat or speak. I was paralysed. At the time I was convinced it was because of the guilt attached to getting pregnant by mistake and ending a new-life through abortion.

The shame was bottomless. I felt worthless, riddled with self-hatred. Since this time, I have heard various stories about female family members on both sides. There was a beautiful aunt who became schizophrenic in her late teens following a failed courtship in Shanghai, who behaved in an overtly sexual manner much to the horror of her parents, my paternal grandparents who I never met. She was lobotomised and lived in care throughout her adult life in the UK. That her pain was part of the transferral of shame I felt, alongside my mother's distress at her own thwarted sexuality and creativity, I have no doubt. I was a weak, leaky vessel, lacking in self-identity. I unknowingly absorbed the projections of those around me who were incapable of processing their own chaotic and repressed emotions. My mother spewed her moods, and her words of distaste and vitriol would somehow cleanse her. Perhaps they did because she consistently used me as target practice.

I had to turn to her for money to get an abortion. She railed at me down the telephone for almost an hour: 'How could I… how could I be so stupid?'

My mother sent a cheque in the post to where I was living at my father's house in London, and he opened it.

There was no escape from the facts as the cheque was written out to a well-known abortion clinic. My father could not meet my eye for at least the coming year; I took to drinking excessively whenever the opportunity arose. I did not even like alcohol; I was primarily a smoker and a coffee drinker. I liked my wits about me. But overwhelming shame begets the need to escape reality.

And no one thought to ask why I chose to drink so much. I could only assume no one cared.

Today I see it through a lens of recovery from the abuse-cycle of an alcoholic, narcissistic mother and grandmother, but here's a primer of what this kind of mother creates in a daughter, or rather this daughter. And maybe goes some way to explain why my ovaries shut down in my 30s before I could bear a child.

A mature mother with healthy maternal instincts is selfless, validates and loves her daughter unconditionally. She parents her daughter with empathy, and attunes into their inner emotional life as she prepares them for independent living when the time comes for them to leave home.

A narcissistic mother is the opposite. Instead of nurturing her daughter, she is self-centred and mainly focused on herself. But rather than taking care of herself, the narcissistic mother expects to be taken care of by her daughter. She neither trusts her child, nor believes in their goodness. She is brittle, controlling, does not observe boundaries, never apologises, or remembers her inappropriate behaviour, needs to be always right, will fly into rages, and project that anger onto her daughter. She frightens her, and discourages her independence. She needs to be the centre of attention, and is jealous if the daughter gets more attention. Her daughter is less a person than a mere object that represents her and must show her continually in a good light, but at the same time she is envious of their accomplishments, gifts, and talents. Her punishment is inconsistent and vengeful, and she often uses the threat of abandonment to control her.

This craziness, combined with drinking, confuses her daughter and undermines her self-esteem. To the outside world everything appears perfect, but behind closed doors the child is exposed to the horror of a mother with a narcissistic personality disorder (NPD).

Now I understand that subconsciously the thought of 'motherhood' was terrifying. By having a baby I would have automatically become a monster because it is the child that turns mother into the monster, never the other way round in a narcissist's belief system, or world view.

My father, a sweet and sensitive Beta, was also terrified of her. He later admitted to me he'd been concerned of her violent treatment of me; the overuse of her hairbrush on my backside. When I asked why he did not intervene he looked rather baffled, and his cheeks went pink.

'Well, Clea dear, you must understand I was out at work most or at least, a lot of the time. Your mother was… is a very strong personality.'

Dad worked as an insurance broker in Lloyds. He was born in the first quarter of the 20th century and was unwittingly indoctrinated into the concept of the 'stiff upper lip'. He'd lived through war, peacetime employment, and an early discombobulated family life where he'd learned to maintain high levels of cognitive control, dissonance, and low levels of emotional expression. In fact, I'm not sure he knew how to express himself. It felt as if his unwillingness to give words to his feelings and pain stopped him from having to feel. And he never cried. Big boys don't cry. Hardened, he encapsulated the belief that the suppression of feeling was necessary to maintain composure and control. I am sure now he had high-functioning Asperger's syndrome. He was a kind man who meant well.

Around age two my mother claimed to anyone that would listen that I was a 'wholly impossible child' and that she was at her wit's end. I was referred to Dr Jolly, an eminent child psychiatrist. While in his office, I built a high, leaning tower with wooden bricks. He said something about 'genius potential', and that I was under-stimulated. It was then arranged for me to go to nursery school earlier than usual.

Back to me at eighteen, pregnant and lost: Naturally I found someone else to fill my void. Enter Henry.

Henry

'You're a really sweet girl, but we're just at different places in our lives.'

I stare out the window, heart rate rising in my constricted chest.

'I'm sure you get what I mean. You're off travelling soon, right? And I need to focus on my painting. My exhibition's coming up.'

Henry pats my knee like I am a child. His cold blue eyes stare unblinkingly at the congested wet road. Strange how what had attracted and warmed me now refuses to acknowledge me. Was it a relationship? Well, that I still remember him clearly twenty-two years later suggests it was. Or rather, I remember the moment he ended it, whatever 'it' was, while he drove round Vauxhall Cross two days after the abortion.

'Your timing is really something. You rejecting me, right now is just…' Further words refuse to emerge.

I can barely breathe. I yank open the window, leaning my head out, tuning him out. Henry sighs loudly, a familiar response, taking me back to a couple weeks ago, when I'd woken nauseous at his mews flat in Chelsea. I made it to the loo just in time. He stood naked in the kitchen poaching eggs when I rushed in gasping for a glass of water.

'I must have eaten something funny last night. Do you feel alright? Maybe it was that rice dish with the lamb?'

His exasperation tightened the air around us. 'Maybe you're pregnant.'

'Ha-ha, very funny.' He briefly raised an eyebrow, while I spun off on my own spiral downwards. I'd been drinking enough wine each evening to wilfully forget my reality. A morning ritual had emerged where we downed fresh coffee and munched on toast; then I enticed him back to his king-size bed. I didn't enjoy the sex, it had caused this paralysed hell of self-hatred I was trapped in, but it is also where I still felt marginally more in control, for some disjointed moments until I fixed on another diversion, wine. And if Henry wanted me—smart, arty, older-than-me and well-connected—surely, I was not all bad. Or at least sexually desirable, which counted for something.

Henry's story was also sad, but I'd mistakenly assumed we'd naturally bond and his initial empathy would continue. More fool me.

The first time we'd been intimate, three months ago, I'd noticed the silvery scars on his wrists. I mentioned it to the friend who'd introduced us. She'd regaled me with the story of his mother's suicide. According to my friend, his mother had thrown herself through the glass conservatory from an upstairs window at his family home in Sussex. It happened during a cocktail party and Henry saw his mother die in front of him. Clearly, he struggled with this reality, although he never alluded to it with me.

Back in the car, the windows have almost frosted in synch with his heart, while my cheek burns from the wind.

'Sometimes Clea, it's better to be cruel to be kind. In the long run.'

I ask him to pull over on Wandsworth Bridge Road; rain spits. I don't even look at him as I gather my belongings. I sense his impatience even more while I struggle to zip my hold-all.

I have never seen him again.

I still get a vaguely winded feeling when I pass that rounded-off corner at Vauxhall Cross that is now entirely different and part of the huge bus depot. A hollow remnant of sensation that flings me back into that horrible time.

Even though it was Timothy who got me pregnant, and he never even knew, Henry got the blame through the gossip mill within our social circle. I'd escaped to India on my year off, and then to university in the USA so I missed out on this tittle-tattle. I only found out about it decades later when he made contact on Facebook. He was still perturbed I had somehow been complicit with this gossip from all those years ago; that I had somehow intentionally painted him as a 'bad egg.' All I'd wanted was to forget: the abortion, the shame.

Henry suggested we meet; I mulled it over but it never happened. Later I found out he'd been going through a divorce. Five years after we'd been messaging, he made a misogynist remark on Facebook about a photograph on my timeline that included a female friend of mine who had the remains of a pregnancy tummy on display. I unfriended him. I considered a written response challenging his misogyny, but realised it best to preserve my energy for more worthy people.

Knowing who to include in this book has been challenging. The more I write the more boys pop up like bad pennies. Undoubtedly that observation will make me sound promiscuous; taken at face value, to be described as promiscuous sends me back to a shameful place. One familiar to me, from childhood through my mother's projection, and then as a teenager when she raged and rampaged about my wanton behaviour before it had ever taken place. However, oftentimes these relations with boys have been nothing more than kissing and some fondling. Checking in my thesaurus I find that 'indiscriminate' and 'abandoned' are synonyms; those two words sum me up better. I certainly was indiscriminate; I was incapable of reasonable judgements about these boys, my concern was to make them desire me, whereas I was abandoning myself in the hope of someone else—a boy—making me feel better about myself.

I suspect my needs and motivations were awry when I was eighteen and living in a rather dilapidated house at 75 St. Georges Square in Pimlico on my year off. A close friend's father was an Arch Deacon in the Church of England who owned rundown houses and flats they were in the process of selling off; I paid £40 a month for a room. It was before taking off on my four-month trip round India—still one of my favourite places to visit—and I made it my mission to go out and 'get off' (snog) with somebody considered cool and desirable by my peers. This was easy to deduce and most of the hunting happened around the Kings Road and Fulham Road area in Chelsea, at pubs and clubs like the 151, Café des Artists, the 666 Club or Crazy Larry's. There was one guy, another old Etonian who was a real eccentric with an interesting energy who I had got off with and taken back to '75'.

He was too cool for the 151 Club—too Sloaney for him—but that was where I had bumped into him, literally on the dance floor where he was whirling like a dervish. He was much in his own world, but I eventually snared his attention. He barely slept that night as he manically tried to teach Boysie, my grey and yellow Cockatiel, to speak while flying all over the room periodically. I myself had taught him to say his own name, but it took at least a month. So I had Dylan going mental all night in my room while Boysie toyed with him, landing on his hand from time to time, jumping onto his head and then flying up on the rusted curtain rail about twelve foot above, draped with some old fabric I'd found in my mother's attic which was now stained with bird poo. In between playing with my bird, Dylan would swoop low to where I lay on the mattress on the floor and kiss me and snuggle for a while. Early the next morning we walked to Oriels in Sloane Square where he was meeting a friend. I remember feeling on this massive high, like I had seriously scored last night and that feeling was going to carry me through for a couple days. I willed for people I knew to walk by and see us even though we had made no plans to meet up again. That seemed beside the point. We had not talked about anything much—beyond Boysie and my planned trip to India where he had already been—but I had got what I needed: a boost.

Years later I ran into him when I was working in the café/bar at a Bridge Club in Parsons Green in Fulham, which afforded me flexibility as an actress. He had come in to use the bathroom, or demanded he use it and it was obvious to me he was off his head on cocaine. Having got off a crystal meth addiction I knew the signs. He did not clock me, but I knew those high cheekbones and emerald eyes. I sensed something lost about him, although he still had that arrogant public-school entitlement. A few years later I read that he'd died in an accident related to alcohol abuse. I can only guess that this feels relevant because after the end of my university years I was drawn to these types of men, probably in the hope of saving them. But I think the draw to Dylan had been his 'street cred', something I felt lacking in.

Chapter 3

Tarquin

The mind is its own place, and in itself can make a Heaven of Hell, a Hell of Heaven.

John Milton, Paradise Lost

Memory is strange: I bizarrely remember the outfit I wore on the night I met Tarquin: navy blue, slim-line brushed cotton jodhpurs, rust suede ballet pumps from Next and a navy and cream trimmed jacket from Wallis, the hemline weighted inside with narrow copper chains, a copy of the Chanel classic once worn by my mother. Oh, and heaps of silver jewellery I'd bought in Rajasthan. I was feeling good about myself that night, which means I was getting a lot of attention from men. I was recently back from my trip round India on my year off and I was about to start college in the US. Age 19, I had a tan, as always, and with a few drinks in me I was the bees' knees.

And here I was again, back in the 151 Club, my familiar stomping ground located at 151 Kings Road in Chelsea. I had been given the dubious honour of a free membership by Adrian, one of the owners, before I took my A levels, when I was gallivanting round London, rather than studying. I'd orchestrated my expulsion from

Kirby Lodge, a 6th form college in Cambridgeshire, and was left with no other option but to attend a 6th form crammer while living with my father in Parsons Green. I ended up at Collingham Tutors in Gloucester Road, but most of my memories were from drunken nights at the 151.

My eye-opening travel experience round India had been a man-free zone, undoubtedly a good thing, but having been back in the UK a couple of months my ego craved male attention. I was at-home within the smoky confines of the maroon basement of the heaving nightclub and I was there with a couple of girlfriends I'd met at Kirby Lodge. My eye was on the lookout in a predatory fashion. I had youth on my side, but wonder now at my audacity; I had little shame when it came to eyeing up and making a move in my quarry's direction. Although, to think I had any power is ludicrous, as the situation with Tarquin proved. But I thought I had power and that makes a difference, I just needed to stop giving it away so easily.

I spied him across the room, leaning at the bar with a male friend. I was struck by his dark good looks. He had beautiful, rich brown eyes with camel lashes, and clear olive skin that made him look Mediterranean. We kept giving each other sneaky, flirty looks that inevitably lead to an initial introduction after he waved (or summoned me) to join him. I was still mentally a swooning schoolgirl. And herein was one of my greatest flaws: seduction through vanity! That a guy so handsome could want me was the ultimate win. I was all about immediate gratification and so was he. Within an hour of having clapped eyes on him, I was glued to his side at the bar.

'You're very brown. Been anywhere nice?' He eyed me like a juicy fruit.

'Yes, actually, I have. I was in India for four months on my year off. It was amazing. I started in Mumbai where I met up with my two girlfriends, Natasha and Lily—they'd been teaching in a school near Pondicherry. Then we headed back down south to Kerala, stopping in Goa and Karnataka. They have this incredible local dance called Kathakali; quite a spectacle, the costumes and—'

Tarquin raised his hand. 'Sorry sweetheart, but I don't need your travelogue, soon you'll be boring me to death with your photos.' His smile was cheeky.

'You did ask.' I pointed out. 'Have you been?'

'No. I went travelling in South America a couple years ago—that opened my eyes. Yes, I do miss travelling, the freedom mainly.'

'Actually, I'm off to the US in a week. I'm going to college there.'

Maybe it was that last comment that synched it for him—I'll never know—but I noticed his interest amp up. He hated dancing, but liked to drink and talk, mainly about himself. He was good at chat and that night I was the proud winner in the ring. I was riding on a cloud when I handed over my telephone number, confident he would call the next day. Time was not on our side and I think that made this burgeoning romance feel more important and special. I couldn't stop grinning on the way home in the taxi when my friend, Hilary, sighed and decided to unceremoniously burst my bubble.

'Oh my god Clea, you really don't know who that guy is, do you?'

'He's gorgeous, I know that,' I replied smugly, lighting

yet another cigarette.

'He's the guy that shat all over Sophie. He treated her like dirt. He went out with her for two weeks, broke up with her and was in bed with Suzy the following night. Even though he'd told Sophie he was in love with her. He's bad news.' Hilary eyed me warily.

'Oh… really? Well, I can't comment on that.' Inwardly, I was thinking, *it will be different with me!*

Having left Kirby Lodge, I'd gladly missed out on the gossip of my year's convoluted dramas. I was relieved to be out of the toxic, all-female environment brimming with rivalry. I had been desperate to escape the sheltered and mundane routine of boarding-school life at Heathfield, after completing my O levels, and being naive, was rocked when I unwittingly became part of a socially competitive arena: teenage girls can be cruel. Heathfield was a gentle haven in comparison. I'd only stayed in contact with a couple of girls from Kirby Lodge and Hilary was one. Emily Dickinson wrote, 'the heart wants what it wants', even if it is cloaked in delusory sexual attraction, dominating logic.

I was on a mission and that mission was Tarquin. And I had a honey trap in mind. When he called the next morning, I set it.

'Morning sexy! How are you feeling today?' He purred down the line.

'I'm feeling good. Actually, I'm getting ready to go to my friend's 21st birthday party in Sussex this weekend.'

'Oh right…'

'Yes… guess what?'

'What?'

'I'll be meeting a Beatle!'

'Really? That's pretty cool—which one?'

'That's a secret! He's my friend's godfather. Would you like to come with me as my plus-one?'

'Let me get back to you. I need to make a call home as my mother was expecting me, but a Beatle, well—can't really miss that, now can I?'

It didn't cross my mind I could have just invited him as my 'plus 1' without the lure of a Beatle, but as I would realise, my apparent confidence was no deeper than a mud mask from Boots.

I arranged to pick him up in Sloane Square. Butterflies whooshed around my tummy as I clocked him chatting to a blond-haired man with a beaky nose on the kerb outside Oriel's. Tarquin did a double take as I rolled up outside the Royal Court in my dirty orange Avenger estate. For a second, I wondered if he would deign to get in. He certainly looked shocked. He quickly jumped in, throwing his hold-all into the back seat.

'If I'd known you drove such a monstrosity, I would have had you pull up on a side street. Some of us have a reputation to uphold, you know!' He wasn't quite joking; I felt wrong-footed.

'Well it might not look great, but it is very safe. That's why my stepfather bought it for me as my first car and if I bash it, doesn't really matter, does it?'

'You can say that again.'

As we headed out of London towards Sussex, he placed his hand on my knee; his first show of attraction. 'Good to see you again. So, tell me about this family whose party we're going to.'

I filled him in and then I put on *The Cars*, stalling the

necessity to keep talking. I'd had a difficult time finding a B&B for the night and the one I found was hardly picturesque—a detached modern bungalow on the outskirts of Lewes. Our room had two slim single beds. I was feeling awkward at the thought of undressing and getting ready for the party; Tarquin appeared at ease, happy to sit and chat in the kitchen with the pretty, petite brunette B&B owner, smoking and drinking tea. It was becoming obvious most women fell easily for Tarquin's charms.

Later we rolled up the drive to my friend's Georgian house and I proudly looked across at Tarquin. He was amazing in a dinner jacket. Debonair and charm personified. He was eager to ditch the car in the far end of the nearby field, allocated for parking, before anyone could identify us. I knew few people and he knew no one except our hostess, Angie, who he'd met once before, to my surprise. Inside the candy-striped marquee, we downed fizz and stuffed up on canapés. I think he was out of his comfort zone as they were not a typical Sloane family, but originally from Liverpool. The father had been successful in the music business and the overall vibe was friendly, but not raucous and rowdy like a Sloaney party. Not a lot of air kissing going on either. This lot went more in for genuine hugs, something I was allergic to at that time.

Angie, tall and slim with bright blue eyes, introduced us to the Beatle who shook our hands and greeted us warmly. I had the queasy feeling Angie was none too impressed with my 'plus 1' as she was not directing any comments at him, just to me. She was a straightforward type so I intuited she had taken against him for some reason. I left Tarquin talking with Hilary, who he'd met with me at the 151 club, while I followed Angie across the lawn into the kitchen where she was busy taking roast quail out of the oven.

'Here, try this!' She stuffed a blini topped with smoked salmon and caviar into my mouth, which I struggled to chew, let alone swallow. I could never eat if romance was in the pipeline.

'Delicious! Although I have to say I have rather lost my appetite.'

'Hmmm, yes. About him…' She looked at me with arched eyebrows.

'What? Why are you being so frosty about him? He seems pretty nice to me.'

'Oh dear, oh dearie me, will you never learn?'

'Learn what? I only just met him!' As soon as that fell out of my mouth, I regretted it.

'Hilary told you about him and Sophie, didn't she?'

'Yesss, but…'

'Well, that's not the whole story, I'm afraid. Do you want to hear it?'

I glugged the champagne. All I really wanted was to sway the night away in Tarquin's arms.

'I'm going to tell you anyway. He just got out of jail!'

'What? What are you talking about?'

'Basically, he went travelling with his girlfriend in South America and she got pregnant. Thing was, she decided to keep the baby. Tarquin wasn't ready to settle down and become a daddy. He went on a trail of self-destruction—drugs, drinking, whatever. One night he got in his car, drunk, and crashed. He almost killed a guy.'

'What? You can't actually be serious?' I pushed down

an uncomfortable sensation in my stomach. I gulped the rest of my drink.

'And he ended up in jail for six months. He should have got more time in my opinion, but his rich daddy hired him a slimy lawyer. Sorry, but it all rather makes my blood boil!'

It is not often I am stuck for words, but I did not know what to say. 'I see. Well, he didn't tell me any of that. How on earth do you know all this anyway?'

'The pregnant girlfriend happens to be best friends with Celia, my roommate from Kirby Lodge.'

I found myself desperately back-pedalling. All I wanted was for us to all have a jolly time. 'Well… look. Everyone deserves a second chance! Don't they?'

'He is everything I hate in a public-school boy: entitled, arrogant, ignorant. Yuck.' Angie aggressively shoved stuffing mixture inside a steaming quail. 'Owww! I forgot to stuff these bloody things!'

'Hey, move over and I'll help… He's not that bad really, is he?' An awkward silence followed. 'Do you want us to leave then?' I asked quietly, not meaning it.

'If we weren't miles out in the bloody country, I would tell him to piss off, but as I haven't seen you for months I will tolerate him, for one night.'

'Thank you. I should have been more specific when I called you about the "plus 1". I certainly didn't mean to upset you.' I was reeling with the onslaught of information and underneath, irritated by Angie's diatribe. For all she knew it might not even be true, although I had to admit it had the ring of truth.

Angie had stopped her haphazard food preparations, washed her hands, and turned directly to me, placing her hands on my shoulders, looking me in the eyes. 'Clea, I'm worried for you, not for any other reason. I mean, I suppose you can have a fling—if you can't help yourself— but don't take it any further than that, please! In fact, I beg you… Sorry, but you're not very smart around guys.'

'Thanks a bunch!' I do not respond well to criticism, even when it is well meaning and I just about managed a watery half smile.

I could not relax for the rest of the evening, although I put on my 'good-time' mask. Because Tarquin refused to dance—too cool?—he sat at a table at the edge of the dance-floor necking his drinks, while us girls boogied round the glitter-balled dance-floor, but my heart wasn't in it. I did manage to tempt him outside, with the promise of a joint given me by Angie's older brother whom I had always enjoyed flirting with. In fact, I made a little show of this, staging a suggestive dance to *Blame it on the Boogie* a few feet from Tarquin, although he barely glanced in my direction. Once outside and sitting on a damp bench at the other end of the garden, we shared the joint. He hogged most of it, and then we kissed in the moonlight, firing up all sorts of romantic expectations as I earnestly and girlishly hoped this meant there was more to come.

It was a relief to take off early, as everyone who knew each other got stuck in and rowdy on the dance floor. We headed back to the B&B, ridiculously lost trying to find it again in the dark.

Then I couldn't find the keys to the backdoor and we had to wake the landlady, which mortified me. I had clocked the single bed situation and assumed we would push them together. As soon as we entered our room

Tarquin stripped to his stripy boxer shorts and threw on a t-shirt. Not a slow and romantic reveal alongside discarded clothing then. I copied his lead and undressed to my matching purple and black lace underwear, hoping I was looking slim, tanned, and desirable. I was still hanging up my hot pink silk sheaf evening dress with diamanté shoulder straps when he climbed into the bed by the small window, with no concern as to my bed preference. I rummaged through my discarded clothes from earlier, searching for my wash bag to nip into the bathroom, out in the corridor. When I returned five minutes later, he'd turned into the wall and was lightly snoring. He was even a pretty snorer.

To say I was disappointed underestimates how gutted I felt. I hadn't brought up the shenanigans Angie had regaled me with because we were both tipsy and it seemed the wrong time. When I had succeeded in getting Tarquin alone and outside, after the buffet dinner, the kiss had fired up my expectations.

I was used to the opposite situation with guys, where they were constantly wanting and pushing for sex; the tables were turned and I was miffed. I couldn't help but remember my first love Luke: whenever we ever found ourselves in a hotel room, we took full advantage. We had even stayed in one of the sleazy ones in Paddington for a night when we couldn't find a friend's place. Even though it was cheap, it was expensive for us. I remember losing my lust as the seediness lurked within the vaguely damp, embossed floral wallpaper. But ever persuasive and brilliant at making a joke out of every uncomfortable situation, Luke talked me round. Clearly Tarquin was made of different stuff and I would have to be patient.

Naturally, I was becoming even keener on him.

The week that followed that fateful meeting at the 151 Club was intense. The initial outing to the party in the country was followed by days and nights together. The only area that was not great, or verging on satisfactory, was the sex, but I was so smitten I overlooked this as a hangover of his ex-girlfriend's pregnancy and new baby, and the horrors that led on from that.

A few nights later we were out at a rave in a warehouse near London Bridge where we ran into a friend of mine, Mick. He was dating another school friend, Mandy.

Yet again I was taken aside: Mick placed both his hands on my bare shoulders. 'Oh god, Clea, I cannot believe you are with that awful guy! You do know what a total asshole he is, right? I mean he treats girls like dirt, you'll end up like all the others, cast off and used up by the end of the week. He's too good looking for his own good and he's a major manipulator.'

'We're only having a bit of fun! I'm off to college in Boston next week anyway.' I did not dare let Mick into the plans Tarquin and me were cooking in relation to Boston. Also, I was suspicious of Mick's intentions because I had gone out once with him, staying up all night on Hampstead Heath together, but nothing had happened because I was not attracted to him. The rave scene was in its infancy and it wasn't my thing; I'd no interest in Ecstasy, as I was recently back from Goa where I'd freaked out having taken too much acid on a first and last trip. It had triggered an ongoing paranoia. For example, having been given Novocaine at the dentist I went into a panic I was dying because parts of my face were numb. My current drug was boys, and Tarquin was my fix.

Tarquin knew lots of people and most times when we were out, he'd run into a slew of them he would be gassing with, oftentimes pretty girls. Sometimes I would mosey up and hover, trying not to look insecure. Once I slipped my arm through his possessively, but he shook it free so obviously, and to my horror, I certainly never did it again. He had a younger brother who was an informal party planner, in a similar vein to the infamous Eddie Davenport, throwing and promoting balls and parties in London, Oxford and Cambridge. That is where some of the many parties came from during that mad, unrelenting week and we were both keen to be on-the-go, although I suspect for different reasons. At this time, it never crossed my mind to have a quiet night in. And in Tarquin I had a handsome, new man on my arm—or rather not on my arm, but at least nearby—who I could show off and parade as a trophy.

Tarquin had a flat in Earls Court, or his surgeon father did, that we sometimes stayed at. Or he stayed with me at my dad's house in Fulham where I pretty much had carte blanche to do as I pleased. That is not to say there weren't awkward bathroom moments, but my dad was quiet and retiring, whereas I verged on bombastic and was not about to let my elderly father—more like a grandfather—get in the way of my romantic designs. My dad had let me run riot since I was a toddler; I love my dad but as a paternal figure I would have to describe him as ineffectual.

The day of departure for college in Boston was getting closer and I was in denial. I had my mother haranguing me down the phone from her cottage in Warwickshire, that 'I better get my act together'. Reality dawned: I was boarding a plane in days and I needed to organise myself and pack. Why was I not already doing this? Well, the situation was that I had planned to apply to Brown and do well in my A levels and generally continue from the success of my O and OA levels. I'd left Heathfield, my safe and happy school, to attend socially competitive Kirby Lodge, an all-girls 6th form college, the one from which I perversely got myself expelled. This act of idiocy would set off a negative series of events, throwing me off course in a way that I could only understand in hindsight. I'd run away on a Monday, a regular school day, to London, when I heard the news that Luke had snogged a so-called friend of mine from Kirby Lodge. The girl in question was blonde, pretty and petite, and confessed everything to me after history on Monday morning, gratuitously shame-faced. This minor betrayal happened to coincide with the news that my mother and stepfather were about to reunite. I'd witnessed mental and physical abuse, from both sides, and the divorce papers were waiting to be signed when my mother picked up the phone to my stepfather, prompted by a mutual friend. They arranged to meet at a country hotel just off the M1.

The events prior to their reunion were bitter; I had witnessed a fair amount of deceit, pain, and mayhem over their three-year separation. It was less the fact of the reunion than how my mother broke the news. She'd arrive to pick me up for the night at Kirby Lodge every Saturday morning in a cloud of grinding gears, brakes and Gitanes smoke. This weekend she emerged from her black Renault 5 all smiles and bonhomie; I knew something extraordinary was up.

Driving away we made about five minutes of small talk, but I could see she couldn't hold back. She slyly announced: 'Johnny and I are getting back together.' She did not even turn her big brown eyes in my direction. She looked straight ahead, adding, 'And that's that.'

'Righty ho,' I said, at a loss for words.

I was expected to wipe my memory clean, as if nothing awry had happened. I wasn't allowed to mention her suicide attempts, alcoholism, and general craziness! She was inaccessible emotionally, unless she wanted you to collude and empathise; after all, that was her modus operandi. But to compound matters, when I first saw my stepfather Johnny again, he also acted as if nothing had happened: the last few years of hell, alone with my mother, had never occurred and the preceding dramas were all figments of my overactive imagination.

I was left holding unresolved emotion. I felt hurt and unheard. My thoughts and feelings judged inconsequential. My acting-out took on a new urgency and meeting and hooking up with boys soothed my inner turmoil.

So the drama of meeting Tarquin a week before my departure to attend Pine Manor College in Boston was the glue between us. I would not renounce my new amore just because I was leaving my birth country. He was keen to come along. I was determined to find a way to keep Tarquin.

My divorced mother and father united to drive me to the airport. They had never done this before and I was already well-travelled, but I guess even to their minds 'going off to uni' in another country was a big deal. My mother commented how shattered I looked and when I sunk into the window seat on the plane, I fell into a catatonic sleep. I had been running on empty all week. The air-hostess had to wake me on arrival at Logan Airport as I'd slept through both take-off and landing. My head throbbed as the hangover arrived.

I was to live on campus in Chestnut Hill, a rich suburb of Boston. I was not thrilled to be at this female-only, small liberal arts college but I also recognised, or my soul did, that it was a fresh start. I needed that. And I had a plan: to achieve top grades in my first year and apply to transfer to Brown University.

My major gripe was having to share a room. I hadn't done that for years and it felt like boarding school life all over. My room-mate was Cheryl, from Chicago, and this was her first time away from home. We bonded along with a mature student, Joanie, who lived off-campus in Brookline. We all smoked and glugged coffee, lounging in our college dorm. It was an attractive campus with beautiful trees, acres of rolling green lawns and sports pitches. From the get-go I was motivated to study hard because I was convinced my future happiness lay at Brown. It was a wholesome environment and I now considered myself more bohemian. I disliked the trend for Louis Vuitton handbags, certainly not the style in London, and I judged the majority for being conservative clones of their mothers. On the other hand, I was on a journey away from mine.

At that age friendships and intimacies evolved and cemented fast. Within days Cheryl, my roomie, knew the details about my love back in London; she'd cooed appropriately over the photos I had of Tarquin: 'Wow girl! He's totally a hottie!'

Unlike boarding-school our shared room had a small fridge and a coffee machine, as well as a telephone.

Within the first week I had marathon phone sessions with Tarquin, hinting he should hit the tarmac to Boston. My desire for him to visit had become a compulsion, a proof of something important, but it was illogical as he had no money, and seemingly little interest in earning any. However, coincidentally, his younger brother was also studying in the Boston area at Babson College, a business school down the road, so that boded well in my clouded mind. It had the ring of synchronicity. The sensible thing would have been to wait until Christmas holidays when I would be going back to my UK family, but sensible was not in my vocabulary.

Both Cheryl and Joanie were excited by the ensuing drama of Tarquin and me. I particularly clicked with Joanie who was four years older. The girls in my year were pleasant enough, but our life experiences were radically different—most of them had never left home before—and had done little travel abroad, if any. I felt superior in my life experience, such that it was, and Joanie was on the same wavelength—divorced, dysfunctional parents, boarding schools, foreign adventures. She was also in 'Recovery' for food and alcohol addiction, something I knew nothing about. She was slim, pretty in a cute American way, with layered, blonde highlights. I was shocked to see her in old photos weighing over 20 stone at a height of 5' 4".

Joanie had an Irish boyfriend called Aidan, although it was clear she was in charge. She took it upon herself to set me up with a fake ID; that way we could all go out together over Boston, and for someone who didn't drink she liked to socialise. I'd gone on ad nauseam about Tarquin, and one evening out in a bar I pressed the point.

'The main problem is he can't afford a hotel and there's no way he can share with Cheryl and me. Well, one night maybe, but it's totally against the rules. I don't want to get us in trouble!'

Joanie shrugged, glancing at Aidan. 'Well, I guess he could stay on the sofa-bed in our living room. For a week… at the very most.'

'Really? That would be amazing! He's really great, you'll love him. Everyone does, I promise.' I was babbling and getting excited. Aidan gave me a frosty look, but I was too exuberant to care. I was desperate to get back to my room to call Tarquin with the good news. Many long-distance calls later I finally located him sofa surfing at someone's house, someone I'd never heard him mention. I repeated Joanie's offer and he claimed he almost had half the money for the flight.

That week I got a part-time job in a Chestnut Hill bakery. My uncle Boris was not happy when I told him this because I was supposed to be focused on my studies and getting A grades. I already had a monthly living allowance and a little savings from summer jobs. A week later I decided to pay for the rest of Tarquin's flight. He said he'd pay me back. I did not even consider the reality of how he was going to survive once he was here.

Chapter 4

Trouble

I stood waiting in Arrivals at Logan airport with Joanie. I'd spent hours getting ready finally deciding on faded, ripped 501s, R Soles cowboy boots and an off the shoulder sweater in emerald green. I've always found greetings and farewells difficult, so my stomach was churning.

Handsome as ever, Tarquin walked through with a large suitcase in light tan on a trolley. One glance told me he was in a filthy mood. I was hit with a sinking feeling I tried to ignore, while I noticed dark circles under his eyes.

'Welcome to Boston!' I did a bad American accent.

'What a shitty flight that was.' He punctuated his comment with a scowl, reminding me of my mother.

He did not kiss me hello, instead giving me a limp hug, the kind you might give an aged aunt.

Flummoxed I continued small talk, while Joanie made sensible suggestions for us to go back to her apartment to shower, go for dinner and so forth. I soldiered on, telling myself it was jet-lag getting the better of him.

Thankfully Joanie's enthusiasm was contagious and back in her car she shared ideas for outings that verged on the cheesy and touristy, but Tarquin perked up.

When we got inside Joanie's condo on Brookline Avenue, Tarquin belligerently threw open his suitcase and spewed his belongings over her sitting room. He then took an interminable time in the shower while Joanie joked she'd have to charge him for hot water. It struck me that I should stock up on food supplies. I had a feeling he had no qualms helping himself to whatever he fancied.

We returned to the apartment laden with grocery bags, while a glazed Tarquin sat on the sofa watching MTV drinking a can of Coke, with the sound turned loud. Joanie dropped her shopping and grabbed the remote: 'Errrrm hellooo! Ya know what dude, we have a real good relationship with our neighbours right now! Let's keep it that way.'

He gave her a sullen look. 'Sorry darling, any chance I can borrow your hairdryer?'

He then proceeded to set himself up in front of the largest mirror. He plunged more hair products than I had ever used into his shoulder length, silky chestnut brown hair. Vanity aside, I had to admit he looked handsome in his dark jeans, pale blue shirt, and blazer. The three of us went to a nearby bistro for dinner and half way, Aidan joined us, having had to work late. He worked in construction and although wiry and sinewy he had a strength that also did not tolerate bullshit. He took one look at Tarquin and knew he did not like what he saw. Inwardly I cringed and Joanie put her hand on my knee as if to say, let them work through the teething phase. None of this would have mattered much if we were not relying on Joanie's hospitality. Naturally, I wanted Joanie and Aidan to like him, as I was insecure and needy of others approval.

Tarquin certainly enjoyed the bistro food and went the whole hog, which provided light relief as we joked about rubber airline food and huge American portions. Joanie showed Tarquin her pictures, from her wallet, of when she was obese and he warmed to her, as they rapped fat jokes; Aidan came in with his repertoire. I attempted to laugh along, but it felt false.

Once we finished the meal, paid for by Joanie and me, she suggested we stop at an Irish bar they frequented. Aidan was keen to go while I secretly pondered what was really going on between Tarquin and me. From the way he was acting I was not holding the title of girlfriend; his lack of attention was embarrassing. I could tell that both Joanie and Aidan had noticed. Maybe Joanie thought a few drinks would break the ice between us.

There was also the growing tension between Aidan and Tarquin. They were opposites: Tarquin owned his right-wing privilege and Aidan was Irish and working-class. Tarquin made a few silly comments, considering his financial predicament, like 'I'll just wait for work to find me', and 'I'd prefer to wear out my sheets than my shoes'. The second remark was particularly cringeworthy, to my ears, because of his sexual impotence.

While Joanie and I sorted the tip, Aidan asked, 'So you won't be in Boston long then, Tarquin?'

'Only a few days. I'd like to see my little brother, check out the sights, that sort of thing.'

'And don't forget, at the weekend we're going to my uncle and aunt's house in Providence, in Rhode Island.' I smiled at him enthusiastically.

'Really?' Tarquin raised a dark brown eyebrow.

'Yes, don't you remember? I told you all about them on

the phone. It will be a family reunion of sorts. They're really nice… and fun.' I had vaguely mentioned this to him weeks ago, but now it seemed like a way to salvage whatever existed between us, however risky introducing him to my extended family, who I didn't know well. On the surface, a weekend away at their new home was a brilliant idea. And it felt like a more fitting environment for his snobbery. At least it was a concrete plan.

We climbed into Joanie's car and drove fifteen minutes to the bar in an awkward silence. Tarquin sat up front, vaguely responding to the sights of Boston. When we pulled up in the car park of O'Malley's on a residential street in the Irish part of town, he made no attempt to hide his dismay.

'Not to your liking?' Aidan quipped, striding ahead.

Tarquin sidled up to me. 'Is this really the best Boston has to offer, Clea? Can't we go somewhere… cooler?'

'Shhhh, they're really into the Boston Irish scene. We can go somewhere else tomorrow night. Please don't be rude, okay?'

As soon as we walked in, I felt Tarquin's hackles go up. There he was looking spruce and sophisticated, while the almost empty bar had a few men in their grubby construction gear, smelling vaguely of turps. Aidan had found his mate and was downing beer. Joanie found us a small round table and we went off to the ladies. Tarquin and I had shared a bottle of wine at dinner, but I was stone sober. I peered at myself in the cracked mirror in the cramped facility, re-powdered my shiny nose and tried to gee myself up. Joanie gave me a pat on the arm, telling me 'it will all work out, you'll see!' I didn't dare ask what she thought of Tarquin.

At the table we ordered drinks. I swigged my vodka and tonic, keen to replenish the round. Tarquin made his way to the men's. I knew he'd be ages, but even for him twenty minutes was long, so I looked around the bar and clocked him down the other end. He stood with a couple of heavy guys, a fat baldy and a tall, skinny dark-haired man making pointy gestures. All three were doing what looked like Tequila shots, while Tarquin held court.

Should I join them, or pretend I hadn't noticed he'd ditched us? He caught my eye, and for the first time since his arrival smiled, as if he was having the best time. I casually walked across to the three amigos now leaning into each other, and guffawing drunkenly.

The fat man, who had a round friendly face, looked at me and gently wolf whistled. 'Hi there, honey.' He leered.

'Hi there. Having fun with your new friends?' Clearly Tarquin had no idea of their names.

'You with Mr. England then, blondie?'

'She's my friend—from back home,' Tarquin offered breezily. I felt like I'd been punched in the stomach; tension seethed within every cell of my body. I was *just a friend* after all that planning, scheming, and stressing!

'Sorry to break up the party, but we must leave soon. Joanie has work tomorrow and I have classes.' Joanie, my new best friend, had a proper part-time job in a bank, and needed to pay her mortgage while studying. I high tailed it back to the table where we waited impatiently for Tarquin to finish up with his new pals. By the time we walked out to the car he was swaying and slurring. Aidan found this hilarious, until we got in the car when he warned him he'd have to walk home if he threw up. I was deflated and embarrassed. More than anything I wanted to be held and comforted, but had a feeling that was not on tonight's agenda.

Back at the apartment, Joanie and Aidan went straight to bed. I struggled to sort out the sofa bed; I felt awkward as it was our first night together. The evening had ended up more fun than it had started, at least Aidan had warmed to Tarquin after the shots incidence—I suppose he'd proved he could mix down, or something—but I still felt wrong-footed. While I made up the bed, Tarquin peeled off his clothes onto the carpet, jumped into bed and was asleep within seconds. I felt at a loss—what had I done wrong? I crept quietly into the bathroom where I went through my meticulous skin cleansing routine. I was burning with excess energy. I had a silky scarlet teddy I had packed in my overnight bag in preparation for our reunion; I felt vaguely ridiculous putting it on.

I climbed in next to him, isolated, lying next to him in a lumpy sofa bed. Eventually I managed to stop my whirring brain and drop off.

Clashing sounds and darting shadows jolted me awake. I sat up with a start and fumbled, looking for the switch for the lamp on the side table. Disoriented, Tarquin was standing at the front door of the apartment, fumbling with the handle. Then to my abject horror, a stream of urine spurted through the gap in his boxer shorts.

'What the hell are you doing?'

'Looking for the loo—what the fuck do you think I'm doing!' Mortified I grabbed his arm and redirected his wonky form back into the apartment, flicking on the hall light and heading him towards the bathroom. I quickly climbed back into the sofa-bed in case our hosts appeared.

I was just snoozing to be woken again by the fluorescent light of the TV blaring rock music. In my panic I thought I could also see an illuminated stream of wee-wee patches that were fast becoming stains on Joanie's new oatmeal carpet.

'What the hell are you doing now—it's the middle of the night?'

'I can't sleep—jetlag!' Tarquin whined.

'Tough shit! This is not your place to do everything and anything you want.' I jumped out of bed and turned the set off at the mains switch.

He now started to do his 'really cute' routine, nuzzling up to me like a Siamese cat.

'Sorry… It wasn't that loud, was it?'

'Yes it bloody was.' For a moment I worried I might encounter a full-scale rebellion from him. It hit me I really did not know this guy at all. I had no idea what he was capable of, or not capable of.

'Come here then, silky drawers.' He turned into me and we cuddled. What a turn up. One thing led to another, but it was hardly the romantic reunion I had dreamed of. If anything, it was perfunctory. I was just grateful that the bridge of desire had been crossed, even though it distinctly felt like an afterthought. Or rather, I was a convenient diversion.

As hospitable as Joanie was, a sofa bed in a living room was not nearly big enough for Tarquin's personality, not to mention his physical and emotional baggage. The only times he did not complain was when she left him on his own while she was out at work. He never mentioned how he filled his time, but I suspect he sat around and watched

MTV. I was in class a lot of the hours of the week and I looked forward to that time away from him as I felt under immense pressure to keep him entertained. This was not the romantic sojourn I had fantasised about.

On occasion Joanie drove him into Pine Manor College, after she got off her bank job, and he would saunter into our dormitory as if he belonged there. He'd flirt with everyone and loved coming for meals in the refectory as a paying guest. (Guess who paid?) He didn't even walk at my side anywhere, making it clear he was unattached and available, or that is what it felt like.

I was confused. The coolness with which he treated me, coupled with the occasional sexual crumbs, kept me pliable. I cringe at the memory. I can only assume I was becoming de-sensitised to his manipulations, or being in a constant state of semi-abandonment was familiar.

Filling spare time was a problem as he had no money and I could not afford to keep paying for two. Joanie took us round a few sights like Faneuil Hall and the shops and eateries on Newbury Street. Our weekend trip to Providence loomed, although I was apprehensive about how he would be received by my extended family. Neither my uncle Boris nor his wife knew me well and they had certainly never met a boyfriend of mine. Was he even a boyfriend?

We took the hour coach trip down to Providence—his snootiness at coach travel did not go unnoticed—and got a cab to their large, red brick house on Cushing Street on College Hill. They had only recently moved from New York City so there were boxes everywhere, although they also kept a smaller three-bedroom apartment on Park Avenue. I noticed his approval of the large red brick

Victorian place and that he clocked the piles of impressive paintings and *objets d'arts*. I felt like I had finally done something right bringing him here.

My family could not have been more welcoming. They are kind and decent Russian-Americans and made a big effort to include and converse with Tarquin. His main attribute was charm and he knew how to work people. My cousins always had plans on their weekend agenda because they were heavily involved academically and socially with Brown University.

I was slightly miffed at the sleeping arrangements: I was to stay at their house, while Tarquin lodged at their son's home down the road. Unlike my parents, the Vronsky's were more traditional and had strong boundaries when it came to dealing with young adults.

The weekend in Providence was going better than I could have hoped. They appeared to warm to Tarquin, especially my glamorous cousin Sonia who was down from New York with her husband Luc. We watched an American football game at the Brown sports stadium and we all huddled under blankets as the temperature nosedived. We ate hot dogs and cheered the Brunonians against Cornell, even though it was obvious they would never win.

In the evening a private dining room had been booked for the family at the University Club on Benefit Street. There were ten of us for dinner and it was a lively evening. While we waited in the entrance Tarquin came close to me and told me how beautiful I looked. I beamed throughout dinner.

He was scoring points with everyone and not getting drunk for once, which was also a relief. He chose lobster, the most expensive thing on the menu, which I countered by choosing the cheapest. I was still on tentative terms with these family members as it was just the start of my burgeoning college career; I was desperate for their approval and already on shaky ground having messed up my A levels. I knew taking Tarquin was a risk, but I also wanted his approval.

We had driven to the club in my Aunt Tess's old station wagon and they asked if I would like to drive it back, to which I agreed. It was only Tarquin and I in the car as the others elected to walk. I drove along Benefit Street when Tarquin instructed me to pull over. I found a gap and turned to look at his handsome profile, but he was already up and out the passenger door, pulling me up and out so he could drive.

'What the hell are you doing? We're nearly back.'

'Let's go have us some fun!'

'What do you mean? We can't. They're expecting us back at the house.'

'Oh come on, don't be so bloody boring! Ten minutes for a drink out in a bar.'

Clearly, I was a killjoy if I didn't comply. He accelerated from the kerb and I prayed he wouldn't crash their car. An hour later, having been turned down by two bars because Tarquin had no ID, and two subsequent stops for directions at a gas station and a 7-11, we made it back to the Vronskys' house. My aunt was down in the garage, under the house, looking through boxes when we pulled in and braked. She gave Tarquin a hard stare.

'We were about to call the police. Where on earth have you two been?'

'I am so sorry. It is totally my fault. I made Clea take

me round the sights of Providence. What a stunning skyline!' Tarquin to the rescue, although I could intuit his charm wearing thin.

'Okay, right… well Boris is not happy. He was looking forward to that game of poker you promised him at dinner.'

He gave her his cheeky, half-apologetic smile and scampered upstairs like a naughty schoolboy. Within ten minutes he was sat at the makeshift card table with Boris, Sonia and one of his sons, swilling brandy, having extolled the virtues of the Providence skyline. I excused myself and went up to bed, relieved I could check out for eight hours.

At breakfast the next morning my cousin Angus who lived on an adjoining street where Tarquin had stayed the night, looked across at me quizzically.

'Interesting guy you got there, Clea.'

'No kidding…' I got up and went over to the fridge hoping that was enough to end the conversation.

'It's really sad about his grandmother.'

'His grandmother? What about her?' The words came out before I could collude with whatever cock and bull story Tarquin had now fabricated.

'She died, last night I believe. He came into our bedroom late, woke me and poor Janet up. He seemed rather upset. I ended up moving my bedroom TV into his room, and finally managed to set up the VCR for him so he could watch a video. Poor guy, he seemed pretty messed up by it all. He didn't tell you?'

I couldn't quite believe my ears. But my cousin was very kind, unsuspecting and vaguely bemused by him. I knew Tarquin was lying and his selfishness blew me away.

'He may have mentioned something, but I'm so sorry

he disturbed you so late!' I felt myself redden.

'Don't sweat it. So how did you meet this guy?'

'Oh you know, through friends back home… old school friends.'

'I don't want to make judgements or anything, Clea, but I don't think he's really decent boyfriend material, is he?' My stomach dropped as my lovely cousin Angus pointed out what was obvious to him within less than twenty-four hours. I felt a fool.

'We're just friends. He's leaving in a couple days.'

'I should think he'll need to go home for his grandmother's funeral, won't he?'

'Erm… yes, I'm sure he will.'

Chapter 5

More Lies

Tarquin never mentioned his dead grandmother again.

Sunday afternoon we took the coach to Boston and Tarquin came back to Chestnut Hill with me; I snuck him into the dorm and we watched videos with Cheryl. So long as he was the centre of attention, with more women than men in the mix, he was happy. Initially I had been surprised he had opted to stay with me in my dorm room on our return from Providence, rather than go back to Joanie's apartment, but then I realised he was top dog without Aidan around.

Over coffee and smokes the next morning, he announced plans to head off to Hartford in Connecticut to visit an old school friend, Rupert, an art student. I was secretly pleased because I was concerned about remaining on top of my course work. He mentioned another tentative arrangement with a woman I also knew from London, whose mother lived in New York: they were going to drive cross country and deliver a car to Los Angeles from New York City. I'd never warmed to the woman, a tall, buxom and striking brunette with a confident, outgoing personality. He had friends in LA he wanted to see and my school friend, Vanessa, studying at

USC but living off-campus, had offered to put him up as well.

Late afternoon we took the T train so he could set off. He was sweet and loving when we said our temporary farewells; he even teased me about being such a good little student. So, from not great beginnings his sojourn in Boston had been a minor success and he left in high spirits, while I felt a tinge of sadness, if also relief.

I stopped at Chestnut Hill Mall to pick up cash when I noticed I was half way through my overdraft limit. I quickly did my figures and they did not add up: $500 was missing.

I ran to my bank and caught them before closing, explaining what happened to the manager, a lanky helpful man. I swore no one else had had access to my card, or knew the pin.

'Absolutely not!' I'd promised. He said someone would look at the video footage, although he kept giving me curious, sidelong glances. I was now becoming frenzied. I arranged to return the next day.

I crossed the main road and jogged the scenic route across the playing fields towards the main study hall at college.

As I ran it hit me. At the football stadium, as my family watched the game, we'd gone on a hot dog run. I had just reached the top of the queue and was reeling off our large order when I realised I'd run out of cash. I'd noticed an ATM near the entrance so I'd given my card to Tarquin, pointed him in the right direction, having whispered the pin in his ear; I'd been momentarily distracted by the softness and smallness of his ears. He returned within minutes and I'd paid the gruff hot dog man and we hurried back to the stalls to dole them out to everyone. Tarquin had even gone back to the stand to get more napkins because chins and fingers were gooey with pickle and ketchup. It had all seemed so inconsequential I had never thought of it.

It was a slap in the face; he had not even bothered to ask if I would lend him money. As I had already paid half his air ticket, I would not have been keen but still, he could have tried to persuade me, rather than sneak into my wallet that I had left in my handbag in my dorm room when I went off to morning class. He'd been lying on my bed, half-dressed, flipping through *Elle* and listening to his favourite Stones track, *Sympathy for the Devil*. I had rushed back from class to meet him to go to the train station together.

There was a strong part of me that could not compute that someone I cared about had stolen from me. I rang the bank a couple times and then went in to see the manager again. I think because I was young and away from home, he was especially patient. Eventually he raised his hands and said slowly and with high articulation: 'You need to understand, ma'm, that there is no way a random stranger managed to access your account. You must have given someone—a boyfriend perhaps—your pin number and they have taken… advantage. And to be perfectly direct there is no way I am instructing an employee to sit through hours of video footage while you come to terms with the fact that number one, you trusted the wrong person, and number two, you broke bank regulations by giving another person your pin code. In fact, we could reclaim your card all together, and rightly so.' Feeling chastised was all too familiar. I left the bank in quiet defeat: rather a contrast to the high-handed manner I had entered.

I confided in my new best friends Cheryl and Joanie, who were indignant and vengeful. This precipitated an opening of the floodgates from Joanie.

'That guy is a piece of shit! I knew he was bad news the minute he walked through Arrivals with that sneery look. Just coz he's good looking he thinks he owns the world! What a loser with a capital L! And talk about disrespectful—he ate all my food and left an almighty mess in the bathroom and didn't even thank me for having his lazy ass to stay!'

Cheryl had probably bonded more with him and thought him the 'coolest and nicest English guy ever' so she felt almost as betrayed as me; more hurt, than angry. As if her judgement had been thrown into question. I could envision all the 'I told you so's' my friends back home would be trumping. Joanie suggested I call the cops on him. If only I had the guts. But I still wanted something from him. I was in 'crush' with him, which I mistook for love.

Tarquin called me that night.

'Guess where I've been all afternoon? Come on… guess?' He was drunk and slurring.

'I have no idea. New York, I assume.' Act normal I told myself.

'Yaaaah, in New York. I've been sitting here on the concourse at Grand Central station selling my Guatemalan belts.'

'Really… what, why?'

'Because I don't have any money—'

I could not quite believe what I heard. He was

referring to a bunch of belts he'd brought with him, from his trip to South America. I'd wondered what he was doing with so many similar tan and colourfully embroidered belts.

'Any luck then?'

'Sold one—ten bucks. Bought a beer.'

'Sounds like you bought more than one beer.'

'How are you? Missing me?'

'I'm missing something. Know what I'm talking about?'

Silence. More silence. Then a weird yelp combined with a muted howl came down the line.

'Are you still there, Tarquin?'

Sniffling combined with choking noises alongside beeps while he shoved in more quarters. At least he had the decency not to request I call him back.

'I'm sorry. I panicked. I know I shouldn't have. That's why I was trying to sell the belts. I nearly got arrested, it's illegal to start flogging stuff like that.' The thought of entitled Tarquin laying out his wares to sell on a station concourse almost made me laugh, but reality bit.

'Yes, I'd imagine it is. So, you admit you took my money, at least. That's a start.'

'I'm so sorry. I promise I'll pay you back.'

'How can I believe anything you say now. And you're drunk. Hardly bodes well, does it?

'You knew I was a fuck up when you met me, you must have.'

'Well, I was warned. But I was hopeful and naive, I guess.'

'You're a good person.'

'Flattery won't work this time, Tarquin!'

'Hang on, there's Rupert. Shit sweetie, I need to go. I'll call you tomorrow. Please, pretty-please. You know how sorry I am. Love you.' The phone went dead.

All I could think about was that he'd just uttered two out of the three words I'd been desperate to hear from the beginning. But he'd uttered them under duress, having stolen $500 from me. He sure was turning into a bitter-sweet pill.

Weeks later I boarded the train to Connecticut. The proverbial dust had settled and Tarquin had been calling me every other day. Ostensibly I was going to collect what remained of the money he'd taken that he claimed was $280. Cheryl and Joanie were still indignant, but now I was missing him. I was touched at their evident support of me, but also wished they'd drop it because I was still not ready, or able, to drop him.

I was hooked in and he was love-bombing me. I had shelved the theft incident; deep down part of me knew I really should forget about him.

When I jumped off the train onto the platform at Hartford, Tarquin's arms crushed me in an uncharacteristic bear hug; his strong lemony scent seduced me all over again. As he affectionately nuzzled into my neck, I wandered how and what had so drastically changed to make Tarquin the demonstrative lover I craved. I'd taken efforts to look my best when I arrived and even though he was not prone to compliments, his eagerness to get me back to his room at Rupert's was compliment enough. He could be sweet and romantic when he chose. He even cooked us a steak dinner. Then Rupert, tall and lanky with a warm nature, arrived back with a bottle of Stoli. He was an interesting guy who was spending most of his time painting and taking in the art in NYC.

Tarquin mixed us cocktails. I sat and chatted to Rupert on the sofa; we exchanged glances when Tarquin knocked back a couple of shot glasses of vodka. Rolling Stones boomed on the stereo, so I awkwardly jigged to *Some Girls* while Tarquin necked more drinks. Edgy, Rupert dialled down the music because he was house-sitting for his uncle, concerned for the neighbours.

Tarquin dropped onto the kitchen floor like a dead weight. He was jabbering. 'I'm sorry Jules, I'm sorry. I'm such a mess, I'm sorry…'

This knocked me back as Jules (Julia) was the ex who had given birth to his son. He continued to mumble, but I could not make sense of what else he was attempting to articulate. I could deduce that he felt guilty. I also suspected he was still in love with Jules. I knew she was a beautiful young woman with long red hair, model-like limbs, and family money. I admired her for keeping her baby, but could not understand it. No maternal feelings had been triggered in me when I'd become pregnant, just immobilising shame. I pondered that I was a victim of female generational shame passed through the cellular memories in our familial DNA. One thing I knew was that both my mother and grandmother carried immense shame. Today I believe that both were narcissists, but I didn't understand that while this disaster was playing out. In the moment, I felt a strange empathy with Tarquin.

I felt sad about the situation, so I went off to bed alone. Perhaps I understood a little more about him; he had certainly revealed more of himself in his drunken stupor than in any conversation we'd ever had.

The next morning, he clambered in next to me, putting his arms around me, fresh smelling. It felt delicious to be held by him even when I had so many questions. However, I knew enough about Tarquin to know that the moment could be spoiled in a second.

'I need to give you the money back,' he whispered.

'Okay. Why are you bringing that up right now?'

'Someone must. I thought I was an ostrich but I actually think you are worse than me.'

'Did I just hear that right?—You are joking, right?'

'Think about it, Clea.'

'What about you? What about the situation between you and your baby son? And Jules! Let's talk about that!'

Silence. I could sense him edging away. 'I'm just surprised you'd still see me after what happened with the money, your money.'

'What are you saying?—That I'm mad to give you a second chance?'

'Maybe… You're desperate for love, I think.'

Desperate.

I left days later. Tarquin had opened-up to me a little about his son. Jules would not let him see the boy because he'd abandoned her so completely at the beginning of her pregnancy. She was uninterested in his confusion and conflict—he'd now been pegged as a bad egg in their social circle. Jules and baby boy were doing some mother/baby modelling and Tarquin felt this was further evidence of her 'rubbing it in his face'; however, I also detected a note of pride. He claimed that because Julia had family money, she enjoyed the control she had over him, because she did not need him for financial support. I wondered if that was part of why he seemed so aimless, and why he had jumped at the chance to get away from the UK. He never mentioned career interests whatsoever beyond showing me contact sheets of some test modelling shots a photographer friend had done of him. But he was under six foot and the camera did not love the angles and dimensions of his features. He had never mentioned university either, and I suspected he had done badly at school, not getting good enough grades to attend, although he claimed once that he found 'the whole grotty student thing really dull.'

Weeks later, when Tarquin had set off to LA, I received a phone call from Rupert. Tarquin had stolen all his camera equipment. 'Tarquin the Trap' became his nickname and we'd moan at each other down the phone. Similar stories wended their way to me over the next couple years.

Over two decades later, Tarquin contacted me via Facebook. He was living in San Francisco, promoting a natural male-enhancement supplement, to treat male impotency; he claimed it was the ultimate cure.

In the photos on his website, he looked healthy and happy. The main photo was of him regally sitting atop a long Oak table, on a beach, surrounded by a bevy of blonde beautiful women, typically Californian looking. He looked like he was running a harem. Now grey, his chiselled good looks and cold eyes gave him a sleazy authority.

His website made me smile.

Chapter 6

Boys at Brown: Two Germans and a Greek

Coelum non animum mutant qui trans mare currant. (Those who cross the sea change the sky above them, but not their souls.)

Horace, The Odes of Horace

My time at Brown University was one of confusion and uncertainty. I had equated getting into Brown to nirvana. My expectations were impossible to meet, fantasies of perfection: good grades, a desirable boyfriend by my side—raising my social stock—alongside a huge group of new friends. I hoped to replicate my first-love experience from the early days with Luke, but my social veneer had eroded in that three-year window, and something at my core—my soul level—had too. However, I was adept at wearing a tight-edged mask.

Having transferred from the small, all-girls college into the sophomore year (second year in the American four-year college system), I had to make friends all over. Leaving Pine Manor was hard; I'd bonded with lovely young women there, but my tendency was to cut ties and move on. I also had to work to maintain decent grades because my American cousins were generously financing my undergraduate education and I was indebted to them;

I should add that was the arrangement from the beginning as my dad could not afford the costs to study in the US, and it had been their suggestion. Adding to this sense of fraudulence, I harboured secret doubts about being the first woman to transfer from Pine Manor College into Brown, an Ivy League; even though I'd achieved straight A grades in my freshman year I never felt I belonged.

However, before I even started what I had deemed my miraculous new life, I received a call at my mother's cottage in Warwickshire, from my NHS surgery in Fulham. I was due to leave for Boston in three days.

'We've been trying to get hold of you for over a year,' the nurse said.

'Really? Sorry. I have been away at university in the States. Is there a problem?'

'Unfortunately, yes—yes, there is. You came in for a Pap smear test, but never picked up the results, right? It's been over a year and your test shows worrying irregularities. You'll need to get treatment, as soon as possible.'

I feel a cold prickling my chest and a vacuum of dread churn my stomach. My mother, who'd been in the kitchen nearby, is at my side, grabbing the phone.

'Hello! This is her mother. What's going on? What's the problem?' Mummy's strident tones, tinged with hysteria, take over the room. The nurse says something I cannot hear properly.

'I beg your pardon! I'm her mother! What the hell is going on? Has she got cancer?' my mother yells down the phone. My stepfather joins the party and I feel like I am about to throw up. I mouth at my mother, 'please stop

Mum', but it's too late for that as she screams down the phone: 'How dare you speak to me like that!' She slams the phone down.

I can't even look at my mother. I am the one with pre-cancerous cells, but she cannot resist creating a drama. It's always all about her. My stepfather has taken control and gets her out of the room. I absorb the facts and realise I need to call back the surgery. I am devastated, but my main concern is to get through to the nurse and first, apologise for my mother's behaviour.

'Well dear, it's not about her, it's about you. I hope you have some other more sensible support,' the nurse kindly says. We then discuss details regarding how to deal with an abnormal Pap smear result, which will mean following up with laser treatment back in the States.

Fear for my health—something I had thus far taken for granted—short-circuited the excitement and anticipation of a fresh, new start at Brown. On a deeper level I knew that cervical cancer was caused by Human Papilloma Virus (HPV), a sexually transmitted disease. I internalised the intense shame: shame on top of shame. I believed I was being punished for my promiscuity and the abortion. I shared this information with no one, and left the UK heavy hearted.

Fortunately, at Brown my visits to the gynaecologist and clinic were covered by the compulsory medical insurance included with the fees. This meant the vile secret was shared only with myself. I'd had a hideous fight with my mother before I'd left in which she'd confirmed my 'slut-status', throwing back the abortion in my face in shrill shrieks, as further proof. Not that proof was needed in my mind.

I had the treatment alone, and told no one; I was so new that I was still making friends and there was no way I would get my expanded family involved. My mother was not speaking to me.

What I recollect most from this experience was the doctor asking if I'd been under intense stress. I could only shrug; I really did not know what constituted 'stress'. He went on to say that to maintain my health I needed to get my stress levels under control. The only way I knew how to do that was to bury it.

To say I felt my new start had been tarnished was true, but I also had a bullish tendency that determined that this would be the end of the problem. Ironically, sixteen years later I developed serious infertility issues. Clearly this—my reproductive area—was to be my physical weak spot, and partly a manifestation of all those buried, unhealthy thoughts and feelings.

I'd had so little ongoing contact with the opposite sex that they were still very much an unknown quantity; I was not comfortable in my own skin and found the social politics at Brown convoluted. My new friends and I all wanted boyfriends, but I think we were emotionally and psychologically two years ahead of our male contemporaries. Hormones were high and I got carried along with the energy that permeates a mixed university campus.

I would sway between girly, bubblegum thinking of wanting to find 'the one', into strident feminism, set off by a mind-opening 'Sources of Contemporary Art' course. One evening at the college bar, during my more radical phase, I propositioned a guy with, 'Do you want to fuck?'

We can all guess how that one turned out; the next day, I felt beyond horrific and pushed the experience back into the recesses of my mind. Part of me found being brash covered a load of insecurities, but I think the only person I was kidding was me.

I dated a Greek boy who was wiry and classically good looking with thick wavy brown hair and chiselled classical features. We only lasted three months. He was a distraction and I ended up making spiteful jokes at his expense—he had a premature ejaculation issue—at a party one night. He didn't speak to me again.

Two Germans followed. The first, Hans, was a proper relationship, while the second, Frederick, was an obsession. Hans was interesting; brought up in Hong Kong, he'd had his heart broken by an English girl, also studying at Brown the year before. I was an inferior replacement. He was clever, artistic, and passionate about an assortment of things such as sushi, art and world politics. I had set my sights on him at his best friend's party, celebrating the toppling of the Berlin Wall. I was brazen in my pursuit and willingly played along. I kept engineering our meeting and weeks later we got together, although it always felt contrived.

Basically, I wanted a boyfriend and he fit the bill. He had a strong mother, an artist, so he seemed happy to be dominated by a female. We got together near the time of his graduation and there was a posse we hung out with that was a lot of fun: parties, waterfront BBQs, long brunches, sushi specials that Hans prepared lovingly for me and his friends. As most of them were graduating and this was their last weeks together, the atmosphere was heady and sentimental, which added to the idea that Hans and I had something worth keeping. He was also known to be an oddball and wanted a 'girlfriend' as much as I wanted a 'boyfriend'.

We planned for that summer when he would be back in Baden-Baden, the spa and casino town in SW Germany. I was to visit my mother and stepfather in the Le Charente region in France so I could feasibly take a train cross country to visit him. My mother was negative about me seeing a German, but I tried to ignore her as she was prejudiced and opinionated about most things I did. She didn't like that I was not turning to her for input anymore, so she would deliberately find something negative to stoke her unruly internal embers into fires.

I got on the train and he met me in Frankfurt where he would start his first proper job in a couple months with a well-known advertising agency; he'd jumped through hoops to win the starting position. He wanted to be an artist, but paternal pressure was on him to take advantage of his expensive Ivy League education. I could feel his frustration, but he was resigned, which I found irritating; his behaviour did not mirror his unconventional beliefs.

There was also the ghost of a girlfriend past I suspected had something to do with his attraction to me. Truthfully, she was not at all like me: pale skinned with blonde corkscrewed hair, the daughter of a Scottish aristocrat. Hans had spent time with her at their family estate, a castle in Hampshire. He loved to tell me about their breakfast rituals and blood sports traditions.

'If she's so marvellous, why aren't you two still together?' I snapped back at him one time, but regretted it as he looked as if he was about to cry. I was not open to male vulnerability at this stage; I never cried myself and the sight of a boy crying personified my idea of weakness. I was indoctrinated by my 'stiff upper lip' upbringing.

Hans looked down and spoke softly, not making eye contact: 'We had planned to marry in Venice. We had been to Poland together on this amazing road trip and she had gone back home for a family gathering. We arranged to meet at our special place in Chelsea. We were going to receive a blessing from a priest we had met there—she's Catholic—and then go to Bow Bells in London to formalise it in a registry office.'

I was gob-smacked; this was news. 'Oh right, sorry Hans… What happened?'

'She didn't come. I waited and waited… she didn't call the hotel, she didn't write, nothing.'

'That's really awful.'

'Yeah… so good riddance. I know her mother got involved and that woman had an iron will. If she put her foot down then there was just no way.'

'It wasn't meant to be.' I smiled at him, gently placing my hand over his.

'No, it wasn't. So, guess where we're going?'

I smiled at him.

'We are going to drive to Poznan in Poland to see my friend Zofia. She is one of my favourite people in the world and she is staying at her parents' place. She's with her boyfriend from Yale—they're grad students. You'll love her.'

I was dubious about how much I would love Zofia. I was suspicious of girls that easily made friends with boys. But she had a boyfriend so that comforted me.

We had an inauspicious start when Hans crashed the new VW Golf his father had bought him on graduation.

We were in a terrible traffic jam on the autobahn heading east and it was a hot summer day. A truck pulled out and Hans didn't have time to brake. He was gutted as the engine crumpled like a ball of paper. We were unhurt, but the car was going nowhere again. We sat at the side of the road waiting for a tow truck. I'd packed a picnic and this seemed a good time to chow down and open the bottle of wine. I have photos of us sitting on a tartan rug swigging from a wine bottle grinning from ear to ear, with a slight edge of hysteria in the air, the result of escaping what could have been a hideous accident.

Undeterred and back in Frankfurt, Hans filed the car insurance claim and arranged to rent a car. He was determined I see Poland and I got caught up in his enthusiasm. Again, we set off to Poznan, this time without mishap, and arrived with bright stars overhead seen through the open sunroof as we sped along the windy roads, *Talking Heads* blaring. Even though we arrived late at night, Zofia's mother insisted we eat—traditional pierogi with forcemeat (beef and onion), mushroom, and a delicious cabbage stew called Bigos with homemade bread.

From our arrival Zofia and her parents were warm and hospitable. By Polish standards they were well off and lived in a 1950s house in a village a few miles outside Poznan, known for its chinaware. We took in the local sights—churches mainly—and I felt at peace. Maybe because Hans and I had relaxed into a companionable duo and our foursome with Zofia and her boyfriend had working chemistry. I recall many joyful moments, which photos bear out.

Alas, the joy did not last. Summer break ended and I

was at Brown with Hans working full time as a junior account executive at an advertising agency. I could hear in his tone that he was unhappy when we spoke on the phone every few weeks. It was a strangely passionless relationship: there was a reasonable level of sexual attraction, but no fire or true connection.

After my experience with Tarquin this was a relief; with him I was often in a state of physical neediness, as he was so sexually withholding, or perhaps impotent. It did, however, feel like a compromise that did not suit my nature.

On my next break from university, I visited Hans for a week in Frankfurt and Baden Baden, where his parents lived and with whom I got on well. The most memorable exchange between Hans and I took place while we canoodled in the guest bedroom at his parent's apartment on a luscious hillside. They had gone out and we had just finished a typical German breakfast of cold meats, cheese and bread.

Hans pulled away from kissing me and said quietly, 'There's something I need to talk to you about.' He looked insecure. I internally panicked. Was he going to confess duplicity? Dump me? He continued, 'It's a little awkward to broach.' His command of the English language always impressed me, just as I found his cleverness sexy.

'Look Hans, go on and say it. I'm a big girl.' I gave him a weak smile.

'Okay, well…'

'Go on!' I demanded impatiently.

'It's your… breath—'

'My what, my breath?'

A long pause.

'Well, when I kiss you… it tastes bad.' Hans looked away sheepishly. I was mortified. What woman wouldn't be?

'Ah I know! It's from the sausage and salami getting stuck in this gap in my teeth.'

I was bent over laughing, from embarrassment and relief. I slid off the bed and skipped into the bathroom to seek dental floss hidden in my wash bag. I had a space between two upper teeth that always caused problems. That I had let up on my dental hygiene and been so spectacularly found out was a little humiliating, but my relief was palpable. I was going to keep my 'boyfriend'.

Even if he was not my ideal, at least I still had one.

We limped on for another year without seeing each other much. His mother had invited me to spend Christmas and I was happy to do so. It was a solution to the conundrum of me and my own mother as we were again in one of our 'no contact' periods.

November was almost finished, and I realised I had not heard from Hans for six weeks. I had already booked a flight, but needed input for buying presents and to give Hans my dates. Naturally I wanted to make a good impression as it was to be the first Christmas spent with my boyfriend and his parents. I had got a job as a part time admin assistant in the music department to cover these costs as my allowance was not matching my living expenses off campus. I was saving, excited to return to Germany. I called him and left a message.

Days passed with no return call. I called again and left another message. He did not call back. Something was up. A couple days later he picked up the phone; I'd made sure to call early morning Frankfurt time.

'Hans, why are you not calling me back?' He said nothing while I fired questions. Silence. Tension-heavy silence. Was he going to make me ask? 'So... have you met someone else?' I half whispered. A long pause. I could feel anger brimming over in me. 'Have you met someone else? Please just bloody well tell me.'

'I started taking this art class at night and I met this Spanish girl, Gia and... we fell in love.'

As we'd never mentioned the 'in love' thing between us, this was jarring— he'd used me as a stop-gap and had now found the real thing. Although I'd been doing this myself, albeit not consciously, I felt undermined. He'd made better progress in the love stakes, which I resented.

'Right, I see. Well... Christmas is off then. I better cancel my flight.'

'No, no, look Clea, why don't you still come? My parents adore you and you'd really like Gia.' *I'd really like Gia.* Was he out of his lost-in-love mind?

I was furious, hurt. Arranging this trip had been expensive and caused even more trouble in relations with my mother.

'That sounds just divine, Hans! I can't think of anything better than spending Christmas with you and your new girlfriend!' Sarcasm exploded, something he never got.

'It would be great. We could all have a very fun time.'

I hung up. What was there to say except that his sensitivity to my feelings was non-existent. Looking back, I balked at his inability to act: to make the call and just end it. It certainly made it easier to move on because I felt he was a coward.

Years later he visited London and was staying at a

college friend's house in Notting Hill. Said mutual friend called and told me Hans was in town and would I like to join them for dinner? I declined. I could tell from our friend's tone Hans was curious about me—where my life had taken me. Hans has been married to Gia for over twenty years. Hans was my first experience of self-compromise, following my head, rather than my heart, although both were clearly deluded. Seeing him again held no interest, although I wish him and his family well.

My last semester at Brown was a warning of what might lie ahead, although I had no insight into this prophecy. The Christmas break following my break up with Hans had been miserable; I had felt hollowed out and unloved, escaping either into sleep or alcohol if I did made it out the door of my father's house in Fulham. I went to Gothenburg in Sweden for New Year's Eve to stay with a girlfriend from Brown, but it was grim as I could never rise to the occasion. The friendship never recovered because I think she saw me as a wet blanket mooning over my rejection. I could not break free from this black cloud hovering round me, exacerbated by my mother's response when I'd called her soon after Hans dumped me.

I'd been looking for comfort, but come to the wrong place. Mummy blasted back at me: 'Don't think you are suddenly welcome here when it doesn't work out with the Bloody German. You made your bed and you can lie on it!' she'd snarled indignantly before slamming the phone down.

I felt abandoned. I needed to escape, before I was swallowed by a black hole.

So I made a new friend, cocaine. I was at SW1, a new

nightclub in Victoria, sitting at a round table on the upper level above the large dance floor with a couple old school friends and boys we'd known a few years. Rufus, a floppy haired blonde and the elder brother of a girl I'd gone to school with, leaned close and whispered: 'Darling, do you fancy a toot?'

'Of what?' I felt stupid, confirming what I'd already been planning, which was to go home early. I saw myself as clumsy, unattractive and boring, like I had nothing interesting to say about anything. I was just another Sloaney girl trying to lose her Sloanyness, but to become what? The burgeoning new identity I was desperate to create was suffering serious teething problems.

'Don't be daft sweetie—what do you think—coke!' He gave me a lopsided cocky grin. Clearly it was working for him. My one hideous and frightening experience with LSD in Anjuna flashed up. It had shaken the stuffing out of me because I'd done no research on the effects of LSD—no google in the late 80s—and took too much.

'Forgive my ignorance, Rufus, but coke, it doesn't make you hallucinate, does it?'

He looked surprised. 'No way, darling. Where d'you hear that? You'll feel good. Trust me.'

He discreetly proffered a rolled-up bank note and a line of coke on the back of a shiny black Filofax, under the edge of the curved table. I looked around quickly, bobbed down and snorted it up. I had only ever seen people do it in films, but I seemed to get it right. I sat back and the euphoria hit. Everything morphed into shiny brilliantness. I no longer felt useless, ugly or unwanted. I was the life and soul, or at least one of them. We talked, we danced and had a fantastic night, helped by a couple more lines into the night.

I only had about six months left at Brown before I graduated. I was focused on finishing my thesis about the British Surrealist artist and writer, Leonora Carrington. I'd worked moderately hard throughout my studies. There was less pressure, academically. However, socially was another matter. I never found my niche and continued to feel like an interloper. I had a couple of lovely girlfriends, but craved a gang.

Did I think taking coke would give me that?—probably not, but it did give me the illusion of confidence, initially.

Boys remained high on my agenda; I was still banging on about finding 'the one' and boring my housemates who persuaded me to get a kitten to channel my neediness. Then I met Frederick, another German studying at Harvard. Now he was different with his Harley Davison, model looks and wavy dark blond hair. He was seriously hot and I wanted him. That a boy so hot wanted me was a much-needed salve for my battered self-esteem. We met at an off-campus party thrown by 'Euro' students sharing a beautiful house in no way like any student accommodation I'd seen before. The Eurotrash at Brown kept to themselves and their clique; still, me and my friends were on the periphery, not genuine friends with them, but invited to their parties. I could never be a *bone fide* member as I was not from a rich enough family. They zoomed round the streets of Providence in Ferraris, Porsches or expensive motorbikes like the one Frederick rode from Harvard on the I95 (Interstate highway), almost freezing to death in the process.

Frederick liked to party at Brown. In the grand scheme, he was an insignificant encounter; we kissed only twice and briefly at a couple parties, but how I let him overtake my mind was an indication of something not right within me: a compulsive tendency that had me memorising details like his motorbike number plate. I had done the same with Hans before we were a couple.

I was using coke socially; I'd buy it myself, for weekend use only, and believed it made me more attractive. About three months later when the few friends I had started giving me a wide berth, and after Frederick blanked me yet again, I finally got him to acknowledge me.

'You do too much coke. It isn't nice on you.' He'd shaken his handsome head sadly, and moved on to a blonde firecracker, one of the best-connected people at Brown for the movie business.

My memories of this time are muddy. My emotions felt shallow and prone to dramatic shifts, often on a whim. These flings may have outwardly appeared inconsequential, but the damage was racking up. I was fulfilling my mother's maxim: 'Off with the old, on with the new', but even she would have been shocked if she'd known how many boys were involved. Her attitude switched from cavalier to puritanical in a flash.

Confusion reigned, but I never would have deigned to admit it.

Here's a prime example: I was set to move to New York on graduation. During the last term I spent a weekend in Manhattan, staying at my uncle's beautiful apartment on Park Avenue. I'd woken on the Sunday morning convinced my future was in Los Angeles.

When I shared this idea with my extended American

family, they had unsuccessfully tried to persuade me to stick to my original plan. Rather contrarily, I'd not even liked LA much when I had visited Vanessa, an old school friend who was at USC, there. Even though I'd change my mind in a New York nanosecond, no one else could persuade me to change it back, even if they were coming from a place of wisdom. My thinking was of extremes. And my experiences in LA would go on to prove what today seems inevitable.

I had been institutionalised so many years, at boarding school from age nine through to university. So I had little idea about the world, but imagined I did. I was naïve, protected.

Along with my burgeoning love addiction, my good friend, Ryan from Brown, died in a car accident. He had a huge heart, was clever and knew how to have fun. He was also gay and had moved out to LA upon his graduation, a year ahead of me. Released on the hedonistic gay scene in West Hollywood, he'd become addicted to crystal meth, the super-powered amphetamine-based drug I'd never heard of before. When Ryan returned to Brown to celebrate my graduation, he was broken. I was sad to see him so lost, but I did not have the emotional tools to deal with it. It made me nervous to witness his rapid decline. He still looked okay with his blond, blue-eyed, well defined good looks, and slim body, but his mind had become slow and his eyes permanently spaced and glary, like he'd lost part of his brain functions. He had been injecting the drug and it had done a huge number on his faculties.

Ryan was like an angel of death warning me, but I paid little heed as I deemed us very different. Weeks later he was dead and I'd just arrived in LA when I heard the news. Like all bad, sad news I buried it within, and gave off a somewhat brittle manner if the subject came up. I'd gone into full denial.

I also immediately found a new fling.

Chapter 7

Jordan the Tweaker

I would rather die of passion than boredom.

Émile Zola, *The Ladies' Paradise*

It was an August morning scorcher in LA when I rushed outside, in search of Jezebel, my cat. This poor tabby had not had an easy ride with me, and the last straw was the luggage hold on the plane from Boston to LA. I had adopted her while a student on my housemates' suggestion—to stop me knocking on their bedroom doors for unending chats while they tried to study.

Directly opposite my Hollywood pink bungalow was a flat-roofed shack a shaggy-haired man was living in; I'd secretly become fascinated by his comings and goings, especially during the middle of the night. Junk littered the front yard—furniture, wood, ironwork and car parts. The shack's roof was flat and this afforded more storage space, but my concerns were street bound and all this junk I had to stumble over only added to my frustration. I edged round the tight corner leading down the side passage to be met by an object shoved about a foot from my nose. Shocked, I jumped back when I realised it was a camera going off. In my face. I jumped back.

'Now I've got the proof I need! Haha!' My weird, scary neighbour hissed at me.

'What are you talking about?—I'm looking for my tabby cat, Jezebel!'

'You're a snooper! You're working for them! I know it!' His wide mouth spread into a Cheshire-cat grin. This was the first time I'd seen him close-up and he was rather handsome with a strong jaw, emerald eyes, and an elegant aquiline nose.

'Them? Who's them? Please. I just moved in across the street—'

'I'll be watching you!' His smooth tone hinted of seduction and knowing. I wasn't exactly put off, but I did think there was something wrong.

Later that evening the shack guy came over with beers to apologise for his 'weirdness', claiming it was part of his artistic temperament. He introduced himself as Jordan.

'By the way, what is a snooper?' I demanded, cracking open a beer.

'What d'ya think?'

'A busybody.'

'Duhhh—An undercover cop.'

'You thought I was a cop?'

'Yeah. Why not?'

I smarted at this; somehow it struck me as an insult and highly unlikely 'Why'd a cop be snooping round outside your studio?'

'Coz that's what cops do.'

His struggling artist persona, living in his garret, increased his appeal; he was nothing like the boys I had known and dated at Brown, like Hans, and his derision of conventional living made him even more attractive. The fact everyone I knew would have disapproved added to his intriguing aura. Jenny, a friend from Brown, had commented on him the last time she was at my place, observing that he'd be cute if he wasn't a 'typical LA loser'. I'd asked her what she'd meant and she'd looked at me like I was taking the piss.

'Come on Clea, you know, the hordes of people that get off the bus every day from God-knows-where who come to live the dream.'

I had thought that was a harsh way of perceiving young people, but then Jenny was a super high-achiever from the Ivy League. I'd always felt out of my depth at Brown, even though I'd done okay academically, and I did not judge other young people who'd never been to college or only attended a junior college as inferior.

'How do you know he didn't go to Harvard, or Stanford?' I queried her.

'If he did, then he really is a total loser.' She shrugged before adding, 'Please don't tell me you like this guy? I know Hans turned out to be a total idiot, but really—this guy?'

I gave her a look that said 'no way' and that ended the conversation.

Ever contrary, my interest was piqued and the idea of keeping him a secret thrilled me. I liked being a young woman of mystery leading these different lives within the melee of Los Angeles. It never crossed my mind there might be dangers in compartmentalising my life; it felt more like a solution to unresolved feelings. I was like a brakeless juggernaut rambling across rocky terrain, jolting from one craggy hill and valley into the next.

Hence, I was thrilled when Jordan knocked on my

door, a week later, to invite me to a party on a Saturday evening.

He refused to tell me where; he wanted it to be a surprise and I knew it would be different. I drove us in my new car, a beaten up, used black Renault convertible I loved. Jordan haphazardly threw out directions while we swerved off and on freeways.

'We're being followed—pull over.'

'What are you talking about! Why on earth would we be followed?'

Jordan said nothing, but was needlessly on edge. He leaned in close, and whispered: 'Any car with an Enterprise sticker on it—on the right-hand side of the back bumper—is an undercover cop car.'

'What?' I started to laugh; I had hired an Enterprise car myself when I first arrived—there are thousands bombing about LA. Catching a glimpse of his face I dared not mention this.

We parked outside a partly burnt-out building; dim light emanated from a basement. There was no way I would have entered a spooky place like this on my own.

'I don't want to get in trouble with the cops, or anything.' He nodded in a disparaging 'don't you know anything' way. I decided to shut up. I craved novelty and adventure.

Following him down some steps, I smelled urine dampened with eye watering disinfectant, along a dark winding corridor that ended at a makeshift entrance draped in heavy, dark velveteen fabric. Edging through we finally entered the party—a large space partly filled with mattresses. Candles and tea lights were scattered across the floor while bodies reclined on the mattresses either chatting or fondling, and others milled about in an energised and goggle-eyed fashion. There were garish large canvases on some parts of the walls and a film projector ran in a corner, emitting grainy indecipherable black and white images on other parts of the graffitied walls. A couple of men peered suspiciously at me and Jordan grabbed my arm protectively. They had a look like Jordan's when he'd shoved a camera in my face and accused me of being a cop. Well, I'd wanted different…

Jordan indicated a female propped on a more elevated mattress with two columns at the far end draped in silks and satins, some velvet and even European flags. Totally bizarre. 'That's Valencia—they had to carry her in. She can't walk.'

'Oh that's terrible. What happened?'

'I think she fell down the stairs. Or someone pushed her. But she likes it coz she's always the centre of attention.'

'What's she doing here? Her bed is fancier than the others, like a queen in state, or something.'

'She's psychic—otherwise known as the Queen of Truth. She's also a hermaphrodite.'

'What?' My head reeled.

'If ya lucky she'll give ya a reading—if ya give off the right energy.'

'That would be great. Let's open the wine I bought.' I have always loved visiting fortune-tellers and psychics.

I drank white wine out of the bottle because there were no glasses or plastic cups. Jordan brought out a baggy and emptied a pile of tiny white crystals onto the back of a magazine that lay on the booze table.

'I didn't know you did coke—'

112

'I don't.'

'So what is that?'

'Crystal—ticket to a whole new world.'

'What does it do? You don't trip, or hallucinate or anything?'

'Nah—try it. Burns a bit the first time. It's pretty harmless stuff but makes you very creative.'

I was in a quandary; how can it be 'harmless stuff' after what happened to Ryan, but then I glanced at Jordan and he seemed on the level, although admittedly different to the go-getter Ivy Leaguers I'd been around for the past few years. Surely, he would not want to cause me harm. I decided a taster would be okay, for the sake of experimentation. And I would stay away from Tequila, although there wasn't much drinking going on, just billows of marijuana smoke.

To be honest, I was also bursting to see what this drug was like. Ryan and I had been close and liked many of the same things, which included music and partying. I justified not heeding his warning and taking the drug as a way of understanding what had messed him up so badly.

Jordan handed me a broken off plastic tube from a Bic biro and cut the proffered line in half. People around appeared oblivious and unconcerned about us taking drugs. Maybe they were anarchists. I felt like I'd happily time-travelled back to the 60s.

'Better take it easy—don't want you flying too close to the sun.'

I inserted the plastic tube and inhaled—Oww! This stuff burned like a flame searing the insides of my nostril. The sensation was acute but short-lived; within minutes a magnanimous energy exerted over my being. Everyone and everything radiated a hue of interest and vibrated a uniqueness all of its own—whether visible in their beautiful hair, delicate hands, original attire or through their unusual, thrilling conversation. Jordan glowed. His long chestnut wavy hair, tied back in a loose ponytail, emphasised his aristocratic features with chiselled nose and chin, while he held court like he was born to, discussing his 'found object' sculptures.

Apparently, MOMA in New York had expressed interest in mounting an exhibition of his work. I romanticised our developing relationship as akin to that between my heroine Leonora Carrington, the surrealist artist and author, and Max Ernst. I had written my thesis about her work, having become transfixed by her self-portrait: *The Inn of the Dawn Horse* (1937). The wild haired woman glaring out of the painting was talking to me, egging me on: 'Grasp life now, devour it before it devours you!' Never had a painting provoked such a strong reaction in me and not through lack of trying: I sat for hours in the Rothko Room at the Tate waiting for my Art History teacher's promise that I would be transported to a new place—or back to a primordial place like the womb—but I had felt little, except stiffness.

Throughout the long evening Jordan occasionally gave me coy looks from under his camel eyelashes and I knew we were destined for each other.

In my deluded state I felt as if I'd entered a modern-day salon, full of fascinating people who wanted to be my friend and lover.

I spoke with Virgil, a man of indeterminate years, who wore a thick python called Angel wrapped around his neck like a scaled wool scarf. I redirected my smoke as

Angel was allergic to cigarette fumes and burnt toast. A thin blonde girl in a tight fuchsia dress appeared and threw her arms about Virgil's narrow waist. Her face was streaked with dark mascara tears.

'She's lying—she doesn't like me!' She looked over at Valencia who had moved on to somebody else. He handed her his drink, which she glugged.

'Virgil, she said I'll never have a baby—never!' It was hard to believe this frail and pale girl—maybe sixteen— would even be thinking about babies and motherhood. In response he licked tears from off her face while I watched, fascinated by their plight. I felt part of their private dilemma, even though I'd never met them before. Virgil placed the girl's hand on the snake.

'Angel's our baby—she's enough for us.'

'No she is not! I want my own baby!'

'Ya seemed to like Angel fine last night. In fact, Angel seems to satisfy you better than I ever can.'

I pulled myself up as it dawned that I was hanging on their every word, like a gawking voyeur, although they seemed oblivious to me.

I felt strong arms around my waist when Jordan reappeared and directed me across the sticky floor to Valencia, sprawled on the haphazard bed with her eyes closed in what I presumed to be spirit meditation. Or maybe she was half drunk and wired like me?

'I don't want to disturb her.' Her thin features were witch-like and her cold blue eyes, which flashed open, intimidating.

'You're not—it's a favour to me.'

'Are you having your Tarot read?'

'No.'

'Oh go on, just for fun.' I gave him my most sexy 'come hither' look.

'I don't have fun with things I don't understand.'

'Oh, how wise—well I'm game.'

A hush had descended on the basement; few people remained and the few huddled close. It was cold and you could see your breath. Hours had passed in minutes. Most of the candles had burnt out while the light of approaching dawn seeped through cracks in the walls. I still felt energised but also excited to give over my attention to Jordan. I hoped Valencia could help me with this new relationship by giving me insights into what made Jordan tick so I wouldn't have another failed relationship to recover from. My heart swelled in anticipation of our lovemaking.

'Someone died recently didn't they—not in your family, a friend?' An ice cloak enveloped me—I thought this was meant to be a lark, not anything verging on reality.

'Why do you say that?'

'Because your friend has a message for you. Wanna hear it?'

'Errrr... I don't know.'

'I'm getting Robin, Robbie, Ryan. . .'

'Ryan! Oh my god, oh my god what does he say? Where is he? Is he okay?' I was overwhelmed; I almost expected Ryan to appear from the ether.

I looked around for Jordan, wanting him to join me and be part of my experience, but he was deep in conversation with a crony; they were snorting more stuff off the end of a penknife.

Valencia took my hand and held it loosely. I grabbed it

back, uncomfortable with her touching me.

'There's no need to be afraid—your friend and his spirit group are looking out for you. He really wants you to be careful. Think before you jump. Oh yeah, and keep dancing.'

Now I reached out for her hand, trusting her.

'I'm new here in LA.'

'I know. You're living too much on the emotional. That's okay, but you need to trust yourself more, trust your intuition. I feel some waves coming but you have a willingness in your soul to learn—that's a gift and you should treat it as such.'

'Can you tell me when I'm going to get a decent job?'

She nodded her head sagely.

'Shhhhhh. You need to live in the present and stop chasing the future; it arrives as we speak.'

The next morning Jordan and I lay in my bed. Time was disjointed and I pondered the weirdness of my encounter with the psychic Valencia. The message from Ryan had confused me and her unwillingness to divulge anything about the future for myself and Jordan had sent a shiver through me that justified my snorting another line from off the back cover of *The Artists Way* by my bed. In the shadowy light of my bedroom, he looked older, his hair dirty and clothes strewn across the floor heavy with grime and sweat. Perversely his seeming lack of vanity did not turn me off, rather I found it appealing. Initially I thought it meant he didn't care and I found that sexy, but as the weeks passed, I realised it had more to do with the fact that his 'studio' (his shack) did not have a loo or shower.

An evening about a month after the party, I joined

Jordan who sat on the curb smoking a cigarette, across the street from my bungalow, where he was waiting for a friend—I have never known a person with so many friends—to show up.

After he lit my cigarette, he slid a ring off his little finger. He held it above his head in the diminishing sunlight where I saw it was made of gold and platinum, plaited in a knot design.

'This is for you.' He took my hand and slipped it onto my finger.

'What for?—I mean… where did you get it?'

'I got it from a friend—part of a deal.' His studied casualness made me think that just maybe it was not a throwaway gesture. I so wanted to believe I was special to him, hence the ring, but his vagueness about everything, including where he'd gotten the ring—and the absence of a box—made me even more suspicious. We had been to Astro Burger down on the corner of Santa Monica, but never made it out to a proper restaurant or the cinema, so a sincere love token was hardly in the equation. But I liked the ring and could deal in illusions.

'What kind of a deal?' I enquired.

He jumped up. He never responded well to my prying questions. 'It's yours if you like it—take it or leave it.' I grabbed his arm and gave him a kiss on the lips.

Another time, when I was still doing the internship and stressing about finding a paid job in the industry, Jordan appeared at my door, late as usual, and sidled in like he was at home. He brought out his baggy to cut lines on a new plate. I was irritated, I needed to be up early for work the next day. He'd long given up on anything so conventional. I was still ignorant as to where his income came from, but was working it out by the crazy all-night hours he kept, fuelled by crystal meth and the stream of people coming and going from the shack. Sometimes I felt he used my place to get away from them; it was somewhere he could still peek at the action from my bedroom blind as he played with Jezebel on my bed.

During my lunch break at work the next day I'd made a call to a drug counselling help-line for advice on how to help someone stop using crystal meth. The friendly woman said there was no way in hell to make anyone stop using and give up drugs, especially crystal meth, which was stronger than crack cocaine and heroin. The person needed to want to stop! I mentioned to her that only that morning the man in question had jumped up onto a dumpster and beat his chest Tarzan-style while he declared himself 'King of Hollywood'. The counsellor had sounded sad and told me I needed to look after my own needs, whatever that meant.

I'd mistakenly thought I'd found what I'd wanted in Jordan, but I'd quickly been put right. Still, I wasn't willing to relinquish him yet, as to my mind, someone was better than no one and occasionally he surprised me, like with the pretty ring.

Another time we were snuggled in bed, one of the few times he'd stayed the whole night. I had taken a small line of the crystal meth and my growing concerns—visa sponsorship to legally live and work in the US, making enough money—drifted off elsewhere. We had sex repeatedly—the drug prolonged erection and ejaculation, which explained why it had become so popular within the gay community.

'You'll never need me, will you?' Even though I already

knew his answer I insisted on asking, like a glutton for punishment, confirmation of my unworthiness. As usual, I wanted a guarantee, a sign that this magical realm we'd entered was not only for this moment.

'I'll always like you.'

'Hardly the same thing, is it?'

'Clea—we come from nothing and we will return to nothing; either you require a lot or you're happy to stick with nothing.'

'How do you define nothing?'

'Nothing…. is nothing. It is how it sounds. It is complete by itself, like a circle.'

'So all you need is the circle, magic man?'

'I am the circle, and yes—that is all I need.'

I'd been unlocking my front door after work when an old rusty, yellow Beetle pulled up on my street, hitting the curb in its haste. A sweaty-faced black guy was at the wheel. Next to him sat a buxom bleached blonde with fine features and the kind of button nose girls pay Beverly Hills plastic surgeons for. She was already out of the car before the driver pulled up the hand brake.

Blondie ran across to Jordan's shack where she banged the door and Jordan appeared. There was no mistaking his glee.

'Twister baby! You're out.' He embraced her, lifting her slight frame off the ground, holding her hard against his bare, brown chest. She was pale and frail, but her hard eyes and angular features declared 'no one fucks with me'. Her large augmented breasts were barely shaded by shiny pink lycra and she wore tight black jeans with scuffed and cheap gold platform heels; everything about her was slightly worn and faded, dated in fashion terms, except her eyes that were bright as glistening fresh white paint in the sun.

She pulled away from him and did a little jig, waving her arms in the air and proclaiming, 'This girl is free and out of the pen! This girl is free, baby and I wanna party!'

Jordan gathered her up possessively in his thick, muscular arms, something he'd never done to me, and carried her over his threshold, kicking it shut behind him as he went, while I forced myself to enter my bungalow, before anyone caught me staring, my imagination fired up with jealousy. And then I remembered a Z-card of Twister up on his wall; she was a porn model and actress. I'd asked about her and he'd mentioned something about her jail time for drug possession. I'd wrongly assumed they were friends. A blind man a couple of blocks away could have sensed their intense attraction for each other.

I had no choice but to retire gracefully. Making a scene would have been pointless and made me look even more a humiliated idiot than I was. Jordan was no more interested in me than I would have been in him a couple of years back, when I was running after ambitious, preppie college boys. What the hell had I done wrong this time? Why did he give me the ring?—As an apology in advance? I needed to forget him. I had certainly ceased to be on his mind.

Clearly an affair with one's neighbour was risky, especially if the neighbour lived in a shack—a tool shed for Christ's sake—with no loo, or shower. And he was addicted to the crystal meth he dealt to support his own addiction. The reality hit me: it was the loo and shower he wanted, not me. I would let him use them whenever he wanted, throughout the day and night. We had 'our secret code' of knocks on my bedroom window and I'd obediently leap out of bed to let him in. I always believed him when he said he had just returned from his dumpster diving forays in the Valley, Venice, or Long Beach or wherever he claimed he'd been, because I had no reason not to and when I rushed to work in the morning the dented, rusty roof of his white van was always laden by junk tied down; I'd been awed by the old van's stoicism.

His night visits came with a payoff for me: Once he had scrubbed and showered, he would join me in bed. He had sexual endurance I had never experienced; in fact, sometimes I wished he would get on with it. Once he gamely admitted he wanted to outdo his own personal record. I found his primitive delight in his own manliness endearing, although I often wished we could behave like a normal couple—outings to restaurants, the cinema, shops, watch videos in bed, have sex before midnight—but it never happened.

During my affair with Jordan, I'd managed to get my first proper job in the film industry as an assistant to a wonderful and kind Executive Producer called Amory Dorset. He was almost paternal towards me.

One lunch-time he questioned me outright in his Southern accent, 'Ya know what Clea? I don't mean to pry, or anything, but I've been noticing you look really tired.'

'Do I?' I feigned surprise.

'Perhaps a case of burning the candle at both ends?'

'Not really. I don't always sleep very well. Insomnia.' I was hardly going to lapse into the details over my midnight cowboy-lover who I rarely saw in the daylight.

'Ya know Clea—LA can be a dangerous place. There

are heaps of weirdoes here; they all gravitate to LA. You need to be careful.' Amory was serious.

'Oh yeah, I know. I pass them every day outside Denny's on Sunset, on my way here.' I didn't add that Denny's on Sunset was where Jordan cut most of his deals.

'You take good care; there's a hell of a lot of wolves in sheep's clothing round these parts.'

'I only mix with my college friends really. I haven't met that many other people yet… but yes, thank you Amory, I'll be careful.' He looked at me in a way I had not noticed before—resignation. Somehow, I knew he wasn't buying it, but I also knew he believed we were all on our own journey and I'd have to learn from my own mistakes.

I did not see Jordan for two weeks. In the past he sometimes crashed for a couple days and all would go quiet at the shack, but I also missed his company. He was a good sounding board for my day-to-day problems and never short of opinions. Also, the time I'd spent with him meant I'd spent less time developing new friendships with more healthy people. I'd seldom seen Jenny after my first few weeks in LA, I had a developing friendship with a second cousin called Mia and an actress, Roxanne, and that was about it. I'd met other people but we hadn't jelled.

It was Sunday lunch time and I'd just come off the phone to my Aunt Tess in Providence who I'd filled in on the progress I'd made with my new job, setting up the bungalow and settling in. She sounded genuinely thrilled. I'd pushed Jordan and Twister out of my mind, and was more positive that weekend than I had been in a while. I realised I was not in love with Jordan, it had been a crush exacerbated by the high from crystal meth that we'd used together. Thinking about it made me feel dirty and ashamed. I'd never used drugs that way before; I'd used cocaine at parties, and that didn't suit me, but what I'd been doing with Jordan was a new and weirder realm. Couldn't we enjoy each other without snorting a high-powered drug? What did that say about us? The seediness now appalled me and I was glad I'd kept our affair secret; I didn't want anyone knowing I'd been mixing with this type of man.

Conversely, Jordan sloping off with Twister made me feel like a fat frump and inferior as a woman. There was no way I could compete with her skinny frame, big boobs, and bouffant bleached blonde mane, not to mention the hooker clothing she carried off with aplomb. I didn't want to dress like her, but it infuriated me nonetheless and undoubtedly motivated my next disastrous affair. I needed to feel I was still attractive.

Walter, originally my landlord who lived around the corner, and now my colleague who'd introduced me to Amory, knocked urgently on my bedroom window while I was hanging up from Aunt Tess. By the look on his face, I knew it was bad news. I joined him outside where he rubbed his hands nervously and struggled to meet my eye.

'What is it? What's happened?'

'Oh God....' He looked skyward.

'What's happened, please tell me?' I knew a split second before he got the words out.

'Your cat got hit by a car. She's lying out on my front lawn.'

Trancelike, I stood nodding. Not Jezebel, my faithful friend who'd weathered the transition from east to west coast after her ordeal in the airplane luggage hold.

Walter, handsome, gay and often bitchy, placed his hand on my shoulder. The only thing we had in common, besides working for Amory, was a love of cats.

'Do you want me to take care of her? I can have her taken away.'

'By who?'

'There's a City Animal Disposal Unit—'

'No, thank you. I'll take care of it.'

I found Jezebel lying peacefully on the yellowed grass, like an abandoned rag-doll. I knelt by my beautiful dead cat who could almost be sleeping if not for the open, red gash above her eye. The dry, thick clot of blood on her off white brow reminded me of dressing our beige pug dog with my mother's hot pink eye shadow, when I was a girl. She must have been hit with incredible force—one sharp blow to the head.

Jordan. I wanted to see Jordan—he was the only one who could comfort and help me bury her. I needed Jordan.

I ran across to Jordan's shack and banged the door. No answer. I banged, I kicked and I hollered his name. It felt like steam was boiling inside, like my chest would explode… with frustration, anger, hurt.

No response. I half sobbed in snatched gasps, leaning my full body weight against the door when I heard faint echo-like sniggers and giggles. I could not quite believe my ears. Twister was in there with him, again.

How dare he flirt and enjoy himself while I was emotionally marooned with a dead cat to bury. The reality of what I'd just overheard prompted me to creep away, humiliated, but also not wanting to be discovered or seen when I was looking such a mess and feeling so vulnerable. Obviously, Jordan was not to be counted on, even as a friend. This realisation deepened the empty sorrow I already felt; a growing hollowness I was becoming increasingly aware of.

Months later, when I looked back on my experience with Jordan, I realised I must have been deluded, or out-of-my-mind, to take anything he said seriously. But at the time, I had placed him on a pedestal. I had even written a short film script, 'Homage to a Genius', about him. I wanted and needed a troubled distraction that he perfectly provided.

My own naivety appalled me: I believed him when he claimed that MOMA was interested in his artwork. It backed up my romantic, gullible concept of Jordan—the great artist—slaving away in his garret.

When the LAPD swooped in and arrested him, I was shocked and scared. If I were honest—not an easy thing for me—I must admit the signs of manic lunacy were there: furtiveness, grandiosity, ego, and unkemptness. Apparently, he had been building a bomb, inside the shack, but I found this hard to believe because he never brought up politics with me and I suspected it was more a case of being caught with a bunch of illegal things he'd dumpster dived, as well as dealing and using crystal meth, which saw him being led off in handcuffs. But then he never gave away his history either, except that he originated from Vancouver.

One evening a police officer came to my door: 'Did you know that guy across the street?'

'Only in passing, Officer,' I lied.

And that's how it should have been.

Chapter 8

The man's happiness: I will. The woman's happiness: he wills.

Nietzsche, Thus Spoke Zarathustra

Stan the Man

You'd hope I'd learned something by this point? Denial can be strong, and I had no idea that it consumed me. I certainly did not wake to the error of my ways. I simply could not understand that these encounters were destroying my self-worth. I was into my mid-20s, but I still held an almost girly delight in lewdness and mouthy outbursts. If questioned I would have claimed I believed women were equal, or superior to men. My vaguely outlandish outspokenness made people laugh and I craved external validation.

Whenever the weekend rolled around my inbuilt antenna switched to 'on', flashing and flaring like an eager vibrator with fresh batteries, raring to get out of the sock drawer. I created the impression with friends and acquaintances that I had an insatiable desire for sex and my exclamations backed this up: 'I want (never need!) a man', or 'let's go and get laid'. It was empty bravado. If a Truth Sign in neon had illuminated above my head it would read: Desperate and Needy. If anyone I knew had ever mentioned such thoughts, I would have probably ripped out their throats. I also found it difficult to be alone. Well, let's face it—like attracts like.

A few weeks after I saw Jordan dragged off by the police, dashing my hopes of his healthy rehabilitation, I plunged into another liaison with an Englishman I also mistakenly presumed I could fix.

Stan had been in LA for about fifteen years and recently come out of a ten-year relationship with a beautiful, blonde Californian who had been supporting him from what I could make out. He was down on his luck (was there a pattern emerging?) and I took genuine pity on him. This mess of a middle-aged man (38 seemed middle-aged to me then) appeared to be in the same boat. To add to his glamorous charm, he had a four-inch scar down his right cheek. He'd known success as an artist in LA and his art work had been used in the film *Less Than Zero*, but it seemed like he'd failed to capitalise on his early success. Over the last few years, he'd been taking painting and construction jobs on film sets in the art department, or building work. Maybe because I'd failed so miserably in enacting an envied 'artistic couple' with Jordan, him as the visual artist and me as the screen-writer, I hoped to rescue Stan and reenergise him towards a committed artist's career.

Stan, however, had other plans: drinking, lazing around my bungalow day and night, and playing *Keno*, a gambling game available in bars and convenience stores. His lack of motivation, low energy, zero ambition and diminished sex drive showed me he was in a deep depression.

I had always been a hard worker when it came to jobs and earning money; I'd had holiday jobs since I was fifteen and I could not easily tolerate someone who would not pull their weight, but I was also consumed with loneliness. However, I also understood something about depression. Stan's version of it was a constant pity party, to which I was averse; he was the ultimate victim-of-honour. I heard over and over about his ex and how she'd done him wrong. She was to blame for his alcoholism, poverty, unemployment and loneliness.

We were together for my first Christmas and New Year in LA. We rented a cabin in Big Bear for a few nights with a young woman I'd met and got along with, a commercial photographer. She'd just started dating a dark, handsome but dull Mormon, who worked as a model booker, but did not celebrate Christmas. Our Christmas was strained as Stan was certainly a *Bon Viveur*, and the Mormon was not. Stan kept disappearing up the road to a roadhouse bar where he played Keno obsessively. It was an experiment to mix us like that and luckily there were no major fall-outs; however, I felt I was constantly making excuses for Stan while my friends gave me despairing looks. The best part was the skiing, something I'd loved since childhood, but I was rather peeved that Stan insisted on joining us on the slopes when he had no money for the ski rental and pass. Guess who paid?

Back in LA, I bought coke to celebrate New Year's Eve with Stan, who, no surprise, was partial. He kept saying he felt awful I was paying for everything, but there we were. We snorted two grams between us after attending a lacklustre party held at Bokaos in Beverly Hills, a restaurant I usually loved owned by an older maverick Brit called Tony. Who knows whether the party was off, or the reality of the relationship was dawning and reflecting onto where we were, as it tends to on these 'momentous' occasions. I remember lying in bed with him in the dark, coming down from the poor-quality coke and feeling the most alone I had ever felt. The strange part was that he had his arms draped around me, but they might as well have been dead branches for all I felt for him.

Stan was undoubtedly a hardcore alcoholic and his drinking sessions bored me rigid as they devolved into talk and tedious stories about guns—he owned three handguns, all of which were in and out of hock constantly—and I realised I was seriously losing any semblance of integrity while this washed-up, down-on-his-luck idiot deluded himself that he was some sort of Ned Kelly. I was fed up with his alcoholism, and that I ended up paying for everything, including rent, food, booze and going out. He always made promises while under the influence that he'd contact this or that person about work, but never did.

After another month, bringing our affair to three months, I almost threw him out after a trivial incident. I'd been running late for work and just as I was almost out the door Stan asked if I'd drive him to and from Blockbuster to rent videos for the day. He pleaded with me and I acquiesced. He then took ages to choose and pay while I was fuming, but kept telling me to calm down and not worry so much; for good measure, he added, 'I was letting my boss have too much power over me.'

I almost pushed him out my car on the corner of Lexington and then whipped back around towards Sunset and Sweetzer Avenue where the office was. Amory, one of the most decent and patient men I ever met, was noticeably angry by my blatant disrespect—I'd not called him to let him know the situation.

All he said was, 'Please don't be late again.' He had a tone that let me know the score. There was already a high level of leniency in our relationship in which he tolerated many of my faults—tardiness, procrastination, inefficiency, and bad computer skills—but we also had lunch together most days where we discussed and dissected old, new, arty and commercial films, which was where our interests converged.

It was a relief when Stan's ex moved in with her new boyfriend and vacated the apartment that she and Stan had shared on Whitley Heights in Hollywood. There were a couple months left on the lease. He was thrilled to go back there and I felt relieved to have him out of my hair. He was so unmotivated and depressed he'd brought me down, and even though I thought I was doing the fixing I also needed to be fixed.

Years later I heard he'd moved back to Bromley, the suburb of South East London where he was originally from, and that he'd become a heroin addict, which saddened, but did not surprise me.

Chapter 9

Brent was Bent

Your body is not a cage. There is no right way to be masculine or feminine, there is only your way. Boy, girl or dolphin you belong. . . When you tear up the rule-book and live in truth and honesty you liberate the world.

Rikki Beadle-Blair MBE, Reasons To Live

Brent and I met through a mutual friend, Julian, a handsome gay guy I'd encountered in a queue for a nightclub in West Hollywood. That set the tone for our relationship, one that was more about a group of druggies than just between Brent and I.

It was a crucial time for me, but I couldn't see that then; my boss Amory had intuited I needed more emotional support than I'd been getting as my moods were so changeable, or just damned dark. I'd promised him months before, having had to take some time off work, that I'd seek professional help. I'd seen a psychologist at Brown for a couple years and I'd called Brown Psychological Services in the hope they'd have suggestions. They'd not been helpful beyond suggesting a list of registered therapists in LA. I hadn't taken it further, and Amory said no more. I think he assumed I was now in therapy.

Walter, his other assistant, teased me relentlessly about my serial mistakes with unsuitable men. Neither Amory nor Walter knew about my binge drug-taking, although I'd be surprised if they hadn't suspected. Saying that, I'd learned the art of lying from my mum, so I always had a 'cover' story in place to back up obvious bags under the eyes, and so forth.

Brent was cute: a clean cut, J Crew type, and my age. He looked like a teenager with his closely cut hair and pale, unblemished skin. He was a native Californian, born and bred in Scarsdale, where his parents still lived; his dad worked as a Teamster driver for the movies. He loved marijuana, fast cars, and motorbikes—he had broken thirty-four bones from Motor cross competitions and was unlike anyone I'd dated.

This seemed to be my formula: as soon as an affair ended find another boy different to the last. In Brent's case he was an All-American, short and stocky at 5 7" and looked deceptively innocent.

There was a vague mutual attraction, but that was it. He even spelled this out at the beginning when we were sitting on the terrace at The Cat and Fiddle on Sunset and he looked at me straight, and said, 'I think it's a good thing we're not in love.'

What girl wants to hear that? Initially I felt an unbearable knot in the pit of my stomach. I looked away at the other tables where the other couples sitting nearby seemed to look at each other with affection. It was too much for me. And then the internal unease I'd been experiencing was replaced by a strange resentment, tinged with an anger that morphed into an ego-driven determination. Who the hell was he to tell me we were not in love? I knew he was right, but there was something so unpalatable about announcing it. I should have thanked him for the traditional English fish and chips, and made my grand exit while I still had a shred of dignity. Instead, I chose to prove him wrong.

Looking back, it's obvious drugs had become a major part of my life. We went out, always in a group, to bars, clubs, and house parties every weekend, which usually started on Thursday evening. Invariably I'd take a wrap of coke. If there was a problem procuring it, I'd obsess about finding some, or picking it up on the way. But I was not alone; we were all hardcore partiers.

I wasn't having much fun anymore. No one else noticed, or cared. Weird things happened, like catching Brent kissing a gay friend behind my back, but the solution became to fake laugh and snort more coke. I pretended everything was a big joke. My binges expanded, and because I was freelance, often with weeks when I was only ostensibly writing, my weekends stretched well into the week. Brent worked as an Avid editor at a post-production house in Echo Park, down the road from where I now lived in Silverlake. I leaned on him, making numerous obsessive phone calls to him in the edit suite demanding he pop by and see me. The loneliness was too much. All I needed was someone to listen. I had reached a bottom line within myself.

Why was I not living that dream I thought I had all planned out?

Brent was decent, if misguided, and often came by to give me a hug and console me that it was just a drug come-down. I knew the English guy he worked with hated me. He'd berate me whenever I called and tell Brent, 'No-no-no, just put the bloody phone down on the bitch.'

Soon after that ended, or just faded out, I committed to a shiny lover I believed would never let me down again: crystal meth. Because I'd been such an undiagnosed love addict for so long—and it was clearly no longer working—it made sense to find a new fix. I'd taken my cocaine use as far as I wanted; it just did not give me the escape I craved, but crystal meth did. A hit lasted hours and the niggling insecurities bubbling under the surface of my consciousness evaporated; I embraced my new lover with a fervour none of my recent men had experienced with me.

Chapter 10

Crystal and Conrad

The journey of a thousand miles begins with one step.

Lao Tzu, Dao De Jing

As well as the serial boys, I was also gravitating towards somewhat dysfunctional females. These were akin to crushes and the weirder the better, although I would have described it as bohemian. I had a new best friend, Marnie. Ten years older, she had a long history of addiction I'd been vaguely aware of but ignored. Impulsively I'd moved in with her at Normandy Towers in Hollywood, a fairy tale-like apartment complex on Poinsettia Avenue where my good friend Roxanne also lived. Living with Marnie didn't last long because I think she'd hoped I could help her with her problems, but as months passed it became evident I couldn't help myself, let alone anyone else. I became more and more addicted to crystal meth.

Marnie was nearly forty and had been in and out of alcohol and drug recovery for years. She was like a hippie-witch with her long red hair and crazy notions. I looked at her as a kind of unconventional mother-figure, whereas she saw me as a motivated and ambitious youth who might help her get back on the recovery wagon. She'd been impressed by me when we'd first met, but that didn't last long. I had rashly moved in with her and she'd kicked me out after four months because I kept disappearing for days, tweaking and dumpster diving, and she was scared for my safety. Men were not much on my mind; I was enamoured of my new fix and the freedom I believed it was giving me.

I was now living in the grungy heart of Hollywood on Loma Linda in a studio apartment that I was struggling to make the rent for. Considering the risks I'd been taking, I was lucky my experience with Conrad was the worst I had with a man, or men. I'd be out and about in dangerous areas in LA, dumpster diving at all times. I had a new compulsion to refashion wrecked, old furniture.

Conrad was a mixed-race friend of Marnie's from Narcotics Anonymous. He was a poly drug addict and a thief, sexy in a gangster-rap, baggy jeans and tight t-shirt way with thick biceps and puffed-out chest; he was Barbadian, English and Irish and strutted like a cockerel.

I was scrambling through a collection of newly acquired vintage clothes when the phone rang. Picking it up, I recognised Conrad's gruff voice, his weird accent of Rasta, Irish and American twang. 'Yo babe, I wanna see your cute little ass!'

'Let me see. I'm quite busy you know.'

'Yeah right, babe. Tweakin'…' I internally smarted—I did not consider myself a tweaker, but an artist living a bohemian lifestyle.

'I'm customising hats actually.'

'Yo babe, tweakin'!'

'How did you get my number?'

'Who d'ya think, Marnie. She told me ya gone deep

into the life.'

'Did she now.'

'I wanna see ya! I'll make it worth your while, babe.'

'Really?'

'Yeah, I gotta a new scam. It's real deal.' He knew I was easily impressed by quick-fire ways to make a few bucks.

'In that case, where you staying?'

'Down on 8670 Martin Luther King, between Crenshaw and La Brea, apartment number 16 on the 3rd floor. 'K? How long ya gon' be?'

'Well—let's see—I'll need an hour probably.'

'Shit man tha' long?'

'What's the problem?'

'I just got outa the can—I'm a bit antsy.'

'Shit—what happened?'

'Just get your cute ass down here and I'll tell y'all about it, babe.'

My heart stirred at the prospect of intimacy, but I decided to quickly finish customising an apricot crushed velvet hat I'd been working on. I'd traded a set of art deco, leaded glass panel windows at Joe's Antiques (more bric-a-brac than old world glory) for a tightly packed garbage bag of vintage clothes, including hats, belts and gloves in velvet, leather, corduroy jackets and jeans, brocade bags, jersey wool dresses, satin and lace lingerie and nightwear. I struggled with the feathers I was bunching into a fan arrangement, and had to cut my fingers apart where the superglue stuck them together—luckily, it was a fat dollop so I didn't tear my skin—and I had about fifty pairs of gloves to choose from, if my hands were unsightly. I wanted to finish the hat so I could wear it to meet Conrad—it's a good rule of thumb to look your peachy best to welcome your man out of jail. I knew he was not 'my man', but pretending was fun; it added a dramatic quality to the evening.

I drove down Western towards Hoover when it dawned that the address Conrad had given me was in South Central. And it was almost midnight. I realised the hat making had gone on a few more hours than I'd realised. I was already high, but because I was nervous, I pulled over into a strip mall. I opened the glove compartment, where I usually kept a loaded-up tile, to take another toot for added courage. I was dressed casually in tight faded denim 501s, vintage leather Frye boots and a skimpy scarlet top with a sky-blue tailored jacket. The hat was my crown, with its emerald green feathers and gold brocade band.

I got lost, but eventually parked up outside the right building. I took a deep breath. The street was empty, but all the droopy eucalyptus trees hardly filled me with confidence. When I opened my car door a dog barked and rattled an ominous sounding chain. I quickly found the tall narrow building and fell onto the buzzer, praying it worked. Conrad appeared—he must have been waiting—and dragged open the rickety glass fronted door. I noticed his grey skin; he had dark bruises on his wrists. I was not keen to be here. The rest is a blur of action.

'Where the fuck ya been? It's been fucking days bitch!' He stinks of whiskey. I think fast.

'I'm so sorry! I didn't have your number to call you back and Elsie called with an emergency—her pit bull Mumba got in a fight with her neighbour's dog and I had to take her to the vet.' This had happened a week ago.

'Come in but keep your voice down—what the fuck is that thing on your head?' His aggressive questioning throws me and I want to leave, but he steers me towards the steep stairwell. The pungent smell of urine hits, combined with a strange scent of burning.

'Who are your friends?' I whisper as convivially as I can muster; I must not let the scent of fear slip out. I note the route we take, in case I need to get away fast.

'He's my cousin and his wife.' We enter a room with double bed, a cot and a worn loveseat sofa. I detect humps of varying sizes in the cot and bed. A plastic garden table marked with brown burns sits by the only window that has no curtain, while a dusty street lamp glares. How did they manage to sleep?

A black man, Freddy, is seated at the table with a cigarette and an almost empty bottle. He tears at the label and barely lifts his eyes to acknowledge my arrival. I have never been into a place like this and I am unsure what to do. It is wrong to be here when they all live together and there is a baby and a toddler asleep in the same room, not to mention the bump in the bed I assume is Freddy's wife.

'Get your gear out then!' Conrad demands.

I oblige, but I'm apprehensive about opening my wallet where I keep my stash in a rip within the lining, because I have $80 cash and do not want them to see it. I hand the plastic baggy to Conrad who does the necessary. I pray it will level him out as I'm not enjoying this weird situation at all.

'I was in the lockup so I'm fucking freaked out.'

'What's the lockup?' falls out of my mouth. Freddy and Conrad exchange a look that diminishes my remaining confidence entirely. My heart pounds.

'The lock-up is where the pigs put ya if ya make trouble—I've been in for ten days.'

'On your own?'

'You got it!'

'Shit….'

Freddy snorts a line and to my surprise goes over to the bed, takes off his shoes and lies down.

'Hey that's our cue—'

'Okay—let's go.' We get up and I grab my bag tightly to me—I notice Freddy eyeing it—and we close the door quietly behind us.

Conrad eases up to my ear. 'Now he can give his bitch a good pounding—Hey wait a minute, I wanna show ya something—I got a new tattoo.' We are in the communal bathroom and my heart feels like it is about to lurch out of my chest. Conrad unzips his jeans, pulls them down while sitting heavily on the edge of the peeling bath. I stand statue still and he pulls me to him, pushing my head onto his cock that is now almost fully erect and very large. For once I am pleased I have little sense of smell left, because it looks crusty; I close my eyes while he grips me and forces me down. There is no choice going on.

'Stop holding back you bitch, I know you want it! Suck me baby, come on suck me baby!' I acquiesce because he is strong and I know there are worse options. I go through the motions, while he gives over to the sensations, then a loud knock answers my internal prayers.

A gruff voice demands, 'Get a fucking move on asshole or I'll beat your fucking head in!' I jump up and unlock the door in one sweeping move. And I run, fast. Things drop from my trailing handbag, but I know my car keys are in the zipped pocket where I always keep them. I never even see the man who issues the threat as I tear past. I know I have only seconds before Conrad snaps to. He will be angry now he can no longer use me for drugs, sex, money and, most important of all in LA, a car. I drive away fast and do not look back once. I thank my lucky stars that I manage to escape when I do.

I drive for hours. The sun is coming up when I glimpse my face. I pull over to take a proper look: I am like a maniacal ghost with streaky smudged eyes and a bloody scab on my top lip with a deep cut. Why had I gone running to that loser, Conrad? The poverty I witnessed had stunned me. I had driven down there blaring Public Image Limited, thinking I was the coolest white girl in town hanging out in the hood. Now I realise how ridiculous I am, while I root out a Brahms cassette to listen to as I drive the empty streets of LA.

Chapter 11

Saviour Peter

My luck changed when I met Peter because he was a decent man who I am still in touch with now. Our timing was just off. I was entrenched and enmeshed in my crystal meth addiction.

Soon after we met and got together, I crashed my old Volvo, an accident that was entirely my fault, precipitating the bank fraud that saw me arrested for the first time. The serious consequences led me to contacting my extended family and entering Promises Drug Rehab in west LA, long before it moved to Malibu, which became expensively prohibitive and full of celebrities.

Peter was eight years older than me and worked as an engineer at NASA. It was almost bizarre I met a man so normal considering how abnormal my life had become; at first, he found me strangely intriguing, but this did not last long, unsurprisingly.

We met almost by chance at a bar called Checca on

Santa Monica where I had arranged to meet with Gaby—one of three dangerous dames of whom I was a member. We had started a club night called One Eyed Jacks, along with actress friend Roxanne, but I'd been too flaky to maintain my involvement. The first night we'd organised, I'd consistently messed up taking the money at the door and generally infuriated people. It was the first time I realised other people considered me really messed up on drugs. My solution had been to disappear into my tweaker twilight world, spending more time with my new tweaker 'friends', fellow drug addicts many of whom I would never have met, let alone befriended, had I not been an addict. I was pleased when Gaby connected with me again, and suggested we meet.

While waiting for her at Checca, I had my Polaroid camera around my neck—it made me feel more comfortable in the crowd at the bar; it also gave me a reason to talk to strangers who assumed I was some kind of artist, which I liked. I was not planning to pick anyone up, but simply reconnect with a friend. I was looking around for Gaby wondering if she'd stood me up. I'd been surprised she'd agreed to meet with me as I was *persona non grata* in her circles.

'Can I take a photo of you?' A handsome man with dark brown, shoulder length hair asked me. He had beautiful hazel eyes, camel-like lashes and a slightly receding hair-line with olive skin.

'Why not.' He snapped a selfie (before it was called that) of us both, and we giggled over the result emerging before our eyes out of the grey-black plastic. I admired how thin I looked with my pronounced cheekbones. I also privately thought we looked good together and he obviously agreed as he slipped the Polaroid into his jacket pocket.

'My friend Gaby is really late,' I told him, adding, 'It's usually the other way round. Maybe she's paying me back!'

'You're meeting Gaby too? That's so weird, so am I.'

'Is this a set up?'

'I don't know?—Maybe! She said a really crazy friend of hers was coming, so I guess she meant you.'

'She must have meant someone else because as you can see, I am really normal.' His comment annoyed me. Now I knew Gaby would have told him I was a tweaker as well, although this guy would have been too polite to mention that. I started to gather my things.

'Hang on! I'm kidding. Well, she did say something like that, but I think you're really something. Actually, I'm happy we met.'

'Thanks, but I should go.' I was testing his interest.

'Do you want go to a party—an early Christmas party up in the hills—with me?'

'A Christmas party—you're joking, right?' I couldn't believe it was December. It had been months since I'd spoken with either of my parents. They didn't even know my telephone number now.

'Let's have another drink and then we can head off, if you like?' Peter suggested. I liked his assertive tone. I glanced at him as subtly as I could, weighing him up. I'd warmed to his positivity and there was also something manly about him. As if he had read my mind, he gently took my hand and looked directly into my eyes.

'I'm Peter.'

Peter found my childishness charming and different to

the women he was used to dating. Playfulness might be a more apt description and it was another effect of crystal meth before the paranoia had set in, in which my adult inhibitions disappeared and fun became contagious from moment to moment. For example, at his friend's party I went from person to person with my Polaroid camera, posing and snapping people—'supplying their 15 seconds of fame'—and charged $10 per shot. The idea had occurred to me while I chatted with one of Peter's friends' and then my enthusiasm carried me off on this mini-venture: I was having so much fun giving most of the shots away for free, everyone warmed to me as this quirky, artistic English girl.

After that initial meeting and the party that he took me to afterwards, we stayed up all night and went to the Rose Bowl the next day, the huge Flea market in Pasadena. He was more open-minded than he looked in his conservative faded jeans and red checked shirt and hiking boots; he even took crystal meth with me, on the way to the party and later back at my place. I think he was shocked by the mess in my studio apartment when we stopped by there so I could feed my cat, shower and change, but he claimed there was something of the 'mad genius' about it. Rather foolishly I'd taken on a friend's tiny Tortoiseshell cat called Kiki, although I could barely take care of myself. There were piles of dumpster dived things in every available space, although I assured him, I had plans for all of it, it was just a case of limited storage space.

I was not convinced I was attracted to him and he was not rushing anything; I felt he pulled back from me, physically, after he witnessed my apartment, but I was unsure. We had spent almost the whole weekend together, but not slept with one another. When Sunday evening rolled round, he went home, only a few miles up the road in Los Felix, as he had work the next day.

I suspected he pitied me, but also found me attractive; a strange combination. But then I had felt like that about Stan, just the other way round. I had no way of knowing what Peter felt, although he seemed keen to spend more time with me.

I took a couple of my screenplays to his apartment for him to read. We ended up reading them out loud together and had a good laugh while we acted them out. What was refreshing about Peter was his willingness to give anything a go, at least once. I also shared my ideas with him—for stories and new screenplays, as well as my more hands-on projects—and he wanted to hear about them all. He had inventions he was working on and I'd sit and listen to his explanations, although most of it went over my head. I had a hard time concentrating unless I'd become fixated and science was not my area, but I tried and I certainly enthused.

We also talked a fair amount and there was no doubt we connected deeply. Still, our time was focused more on 'doing' than intense self-revelation. It was a substantial relief to be with a grown man not dreaming up some impossible scam to get him out of the hole he'd dug for himself. I knew I was not yet in love with Peter—my armour was too thick—but he was chipping away to something still vaguely human within me and I was gently succumbing. We had slept together after our third meeting and he was a sensitive lover; I felt something within me restored after the violent incident with Conrad.

I knew I was not just a female object to him.

There was, however, a white elephant in the room neither of us was talking about; it was certainly not going to be me bringing up the subject of my addiction to crystal meth. I guess I hoped he somehow had not noticed!

A couple days before Christmas, Peter took me out to dinner at Musso and Franks, the Hollywood landmark. He reckoned a square meal might do me good. I had forgotten how delicious a rare steak and chips could taste with some Merlot. I really liked him and I think he liked me. For the first time in years, I was experiencing something genuine, not based on a frenetic crash and burn cycle. But I was also weirdly suspended from feeling too much at all. I suppose he gave me a semblance of normality for the few hours when we met up during the occasional weekday evening for dinner, or over the weekend.

After the dinner, he drove me back to my apartment and I choked up when he declined my offer of a brandy eggnog.

'No, sorry. I've got an early start. I also need to pack for the holidays.'

Peter gently shrugged and looked keen to get on his way. This threw me. I had anticipated we would at least spend the night together because he was away for two weeks over Christmas. Moreover, he was spending New Years with an ex, camping at Yosemite. I had waved it away casually when he'd announced his plans, made months before we'd met, but internally I was seething with jealousy.

'Okay. Well, whatever, thanks for dinner. Happy Christmas!" I forced levity into my flat tones.

'Oh my god, Clee-Clee, I nearly forgot! I've got you something. It's in the jeep.' I loved his affectionate nickname. While he went out to his car, I toyed with taking off my clothes and trying to seduce him into staying, but then he reappeared looking sheepish.

'It's only small, but I think you'll like it. Oh yes, and there's a… card.' He handed over a small parcel, gift wrapped in pink tissue paper and gold curled ribbon, along with a card. I was so surprised and touched I handled the parcel like a little bird with a broken wing. I had no words to express my joy.

'There's a note inside the card. I hope it doesn't. . .' His voice trailed off while he gave me a goofy smile. He then leaned in, and we had a parting, lingering kiss. I worried I hadn't even thought to get him a present, but figured I'd sort something out for when he returned.

When I was sure he'd driven away I delicately opened the present. Inside the tissue paper sat a small red velvet box. Inside the box was a beautiful antique silver charm bracelet with tiny models of worldwide landmarks, like the Pyramids, Eiffel Tower, Big Ben, and the Coliseum. I was delighted and tore open the card and a folded square of paper dropped onto the counter.

It was a letter:

I haven't been able to get you off my mind and my gut instinct told me to write this letter even when common sense told me not to… My perceptions, which I trust religiously, tell me that you are an uncommonly, intensely gifted woman.

Honey, I really think you are 'one in a million'. Is that crazy? I barely know you. I'm not going to go into all the fine details of why I know you are so unique, I've relived those over and over in my mind trying to find out why I sense this and discovered that you cannot rationalize, either accept it or dismiss it. I accept that you are truly blessed in indescribable ways.

(Pretty heady stuff, but I knew where it was heading:)

You had fucked up encounters with 'certain' people who, for various reasons, lack (either always or sporadically) basic human traits such as compassion, caring, respect, pride, etc… How you got yourself into this circumstance I can only guess. Probably an over bright, uniquely different young kid trying to find herself. Risk-taking for the sake of education. Doing things others would label 'crazy'. Naively trusting in human nature…

I wish I had known you before these episodes to get a feeling of how you got to your present state. In my mind's eye I picture a beautiful, wonderful open-minded happy person that is a Godsend to any life she touches. That was then.

(Part of me thought he was crazier than me.)

Things I see in you, subtle and obvious, tell me of the person you are meant to be, the person I know you are… I come along, spend 2½ days with you and am amazed at how you have structured your life. It is part genius type crazy, part crazy, part running away, all energy—some of it channelled—and it is built on inspiration, tenacity, hard work, vision and inner conflicts.

To me it is literally amazing, even inspiring but unfortunately also very sad. The conflicts have too much influence. They are taking away your structure and chipping away at your mental and physical health… I want to help you get on with life as it was meant to be… I know I can help you but the will to do it has to come from you.

In a way I feel like an asshole saying all this, I step into your life for a while then have the audacity to suggest I help rearrange it. I have nothing to lose by writing this, though. We wouldn't be friends, anyway. I could not stand by while a person like yourself struggles through such rough times alone. I don't know how your current set of friends do it. I'm willing to start a relationship with you based on cultivating and healing if you are dead serious about coming to terms with yourself and making adjustments and changes. It would be emotionally very taxing on us both, but positive changes never come without struggle… Think it over carefully, Clea precious.

Naturally I was pleased by Peter's unexpected praise, warmth, care and concern expressed in his letter, but I wasn't ready to quit crystal meth. Lovely ideas, but in reality?

I had no plans for Christmas and I was overwhelmed with feelings of abandonment. I'd put in a reverse-charges call to my mother in France, and confessed to her I had a drug problem. She'd responded: 'I hope you're not expecting me to pay for your flight back for Christmas.'

She then tasked my godfather in London to call me and try and get to the root of things. This was a man I'd not seen in years, and we'd never had a close relationship, let alone rapport. That was one awkward long-distance conversation.

The irony had struck me because I'd been craving a decent, loving relationship for years and when it looked possible,

I was too into my drugs to appreciate what Peter had offered me. He'd made it clear he was not committing to me unless I got off meth.

I gleaned what pleasure I could from Peter's words, but spent the next weeks with my hardcore tweaker friends and almost forgot him. My paranoia was amping up, partly caused by meth use but also because it was weirdly addicting in itself: I was the centre of a self-created drama. I messed up everything I touched like a reverse genie. Part of me foresaw the crash, but rather than ask for help, I battled on, swept up in supposedly fool-proof scams.

I ended up falling for a stupid plan to cash 'washed' cheques; cheques stolen from the rubbish in the bank's dumpster round the back. I'd been successful once, but on my second attempt I was arrested. Having never been arrested previously, I was disgusted with myself.

I enrolled at Promises Rehab in West LA, and Peter re-entered the frame. He'd never entirely left, but we'd not got back on track after Christmas. For starters, I was even thinner and losing more hair. Days into his return to work I'd crashed my Volvo, and in a panic, called him at work. I'd spoken with one of his colleagues who refused to put me through. Then I'd screamed at her. He was angry about that.

He was a saviour. He found my cat Kiki when I checked in to Promises. My care of her had been disturbingly errant and I couldn't find her when my cousin Mia showed up to drive me over to Barrington Avenue where Promises was then located, before it became the more luxe version in Malibu. I'd been highly concerned and for hours Peter had searched the streets around my apartment that evening; luckily, he found her and took her home with him.

I relapsed back onto meth about four months after the primary treatment at Promises. I'd been in a sober-living bungalow in Venice. Many issues riled me; I think that part of my problem was an inner fury at my parents for not making the effort to come out to family week at Promises; I was the only patient who had no family present, which reflected how I'd always felt: abandoned.

I guess I also figured I could use drugs more successfully now, as I'd learned from going to rehab and meeting more experienced addicts. Things like how to cheat a urine test. Once I was using again, I fell hard for a man called Ajax. *Tweaking the Dream* accounts for this time: deluded and consumed with user-guilt (rehab ruined the fun of 'using' on most levels, although memory can be convenient).

Chapter 12

Lucky Nate

To love is to be vulnerable.

C.S. Lewis, *The Four Loves*

I had been back in London a year when I met Nate. My return was dramatic: my escalating paranoia, under the influence of meth, saw me sectioned my second day home. Once the drugs wore off, I persuaded a medical panel at the Jordon Hospital, a mental health institution based in Victoria in central London, that I was not a danger to myself or others. However, I had been on the way to developing schizophrenia, hearing voices, believing that I was wanted dead and so forth. Crystal meth was unavailable in the UK in the mid-90s, which precipitated a healing journey of recovery. For the most part, I looked normal, but there was underlying mental damage that would rear up from time to time. Damage on top of damage! My mother ignored me during this period.

The geographical shift allowed me to wipe my slate clean. I had fast become the queen of bullshit, such an accomplished liar I believed some of my own lies. The biggest lie was that I'd had success as an LA actress. In truth, I'd played a 50s diner waitress in a Budweiser commercial. It was the mid-90s, before the internet and Google—I told a young director I'd had a small part in a well-known Hollywood film. I'd not factored in the reality that he could rent it on video and check me out, which he did. I then lied more claiming the scene had been cut from the European version. This cringeworthy anecdote is an indication of where my head was.

But considering I'd managed to avoid a two-year prison sentence in LA, and escaped a diagnosis of schizophrenia by the skin of my damaged teeth, some might say I was in rather good shape. I'd managed to get photographic work for the photo stories in the ragtops—Jackie's cheating on her boyfriend with the milkman Kevin—and an inexperienced acting agent, who was better than no agent, or at least so I thought.

When you get involved with drugs that markedly change your personality you develop other handicaps, sometimes as defence mechanisms. I felt ashamed and stupid that I'd destroyed my life so spectacularly. Feeding into that was the reality that I'd been fortunate in aspects of my life, like having wealthy American cousins willing to help pay my university fees and then my stint in a treatment centre. That I'd got clean off crystal meth and relapsed and got into even more trouble, with the law, compounded my disgrace. I felt that if I got away with lying about my acting experience at least I'd managed to leave LA with something positive. Confused?—Obviously!

The acting agency I joined organised a social at a pub in the west end and there I got talking to another actor called Finlay who had a sketch comedy group that needed a female player. It was a group of four men and one female. That appealed and I jumped at the opportunity when Finlay asked me to audition the next evening. It was quite a journey across London from Parsons Green to Stoke Newington in East London, in fact I'd never heard of it or been there before. I met the group in the front room of a terrace house, belonging to John, who worked in the day time as a solicitor. It was a casual interview process—five quite excitable men, constantly talking over each other while imbibing red wine, four being part of the comedy sketch group and the older, bespectacled Phillip, directing. We read through strange and interesting sketches, and my interpretations seemed adequate. The sketches were surreal and not very funny, to my mind, but I said they were marvellous and was happy when they asked me to come on board. They turned out to be an eclectic and decent group, although there was a war of male egos that frankly went over my head, probably because I was more nervous about getting my lines and blocking right when we met to rehearse. Then we were released on the paying public.

There was a young comedian, a character comic who was going to MC our show and do his routine as part of the performance at The Rheingold Club. I had been told how brilliant this guy was although I had not really thought about his input much, as I was concerned with the smooth-running of the sequence of sketches once in the venue as well as the costume changes in such a tiny space, surrounded by only men. Having had little live performance experience, I was nervous. I couldn't let that show, as it would have belied my original lies about my experience.

I couldn't help noticing the strong, chiselled Nigerian

features of Nate while he stood at the bar, drinking a beer. He was dressed in his comic character's dapper 70s silver grey suit, with his braided hair falling to his shoulders. To my eyes he cut a dissolute, romantic picture as he had a worn expression, exacerbated by his tired, blood-shot eyes conjuring long, dark nights of the soul. He did turn out to be romantic and slightly tortured, but also somehow straight forward.

Mickey, the self-designated head of our troupe, introduced us. 'Here he is—the man of the moment. How are you old fella?' They shook hands briefly. 'And here is Clea, she's taken over from Laura.'

I extended my hand, now visibly shaking. 'Too much coffee!' I weakly joked. 'I'm good, yeah good, just been performing in Croydon most of last week. Delightful as you can imagine.' I was particularly self-conscious, so I was relieved Mickey was called away to take care of a technical hold-up.

'Fancy a drink?'

'Oh no thanks, I'll wait till after the show. I'm rather nervous, this isn't really my kind of thing.' I smiled awkwardly, shrugging, wondering if I should find something to take me away.

'I get really nervous, too. This helps!' He indicated his beer.

'It would ruin my focus.'

'You'll be great, don't worry. What's the worst that can happen?'

'No one laughs!'

'Right. I'm used to that. Now that depends on the mood of the crowd, if they're with you or against you. I can do the same material night after night and get a totally different response each time.'

'Really?'

'Anyway, all the men's eyes will be on you, so I wouldn't worry.' And he gave me a friendly wink. 'Well mine certainly will.'

I was so caught up in my nerves it took longer than a split second to realise he'd paid me a compliment. I felt my face redden and hurried off to the stage where everyone was getting ready for one last rehearsal before showtime in a couple of hours.

'See! It went well, right? Knew you'd be a natural!' Nate looked like he was going to give me a hug, thought better of it and offered me a drink instead. I felt so instantly comfortable around him it was almost spooky. I'd got a shock when he'd appeared on stage with the pink afro wig, but his comic delivery and timing were impeccable. I was impressed. I could tell the attraction was mutual, although unusually for me, I had been attracted more by his personality than looks.

There had been a mixed response to the show. The humour was not to everyone's taste, so Mickey and the others were hitting the bar hard, drowning memories of the lacklustre applause. Mickey's brother had been particularly unkind, telling him not to give up his day job.

Unlike some performers, Nate genuinely listened; it was a strange moment of recognition for me and I found myself being more honest than usual. He was a couple years younger than me and not experienced in love or sex. Or rather, in comparison to me he was an innocent. I had not been thinking about love and relationships much since LA. But the focus I received from Nate reminded me how lonely I was inside. And he was gentle and kind. He was not my usual type, but this monumentally struck me as a good idea. Once we'd finished drinks I'd invited him to a Christmas party planned at my house for a week's time.

I had an Australian girl renting the third bedroom in our house in Fulham who I had met at a rave, it being the tail end of that era. Kelly was a striking brunette who I developed a quick flash friendship with lasting a couple years; she was a visual artist who supported herself through supply teaching and was a lot of fun. We masterminded the party and there was an eclectic mix of people in attendance. I had lost touch or rather been rejected by most of my old school friends because whenever I had seen them, I had either been insulting, a tad defensive and/or weird. This hurt, but it somehow fit my desire to recreate my identity, shaky as it was. I felt I had out-lived these school friends because I'd gone to the US and taken my strange trip over to the dark side. As much as my touches of off-the-wall thinking and behaviour alienated them, their conventional lives did the same for me. Their aspirations struck me as hideously pedestrian. Not that I had any clear idea what I wanted, but it was not what they had. Hence, I was happy to make and collect new friends, something I have always been good at.

Kelly had video-taped the sketch show so we had a screening for those involved before the party kicked off. As I had been arrested, sectioned, and detained in the Gordon hospital the year before, I was determined to make this Christmas a marked improvement, although no one except Kelly, a couple school friends and an old college friend named Alex, knew about any of this. Kelly's sunny disposition created an air of excitement. She was not prone to self-obsession; she loved to party, but was not a habitual drug user or drinker running from herself, like me.

We had created our Moscow Mule concoction alongside finger food, and I was quietly hoping Nate would come. Because I felt more in the driving seat versus my usual passenger seat, I was relatively calm and confident. I never clocked this then, but hindsight is 20/20. I wore an embroidered black shift dress with velvet red heels.

Nate knocked at my door dressed in khakis and a cool anorak. It was near the end of the screening, which he seemed relieved about missing; although I thought he was the most naturally funny between all of us. He was almost uncomfortable with praise and being thrust into the spotlight, unlike tall and handsome Mickey who craved it. He'd incidentally already hooked up for one night with Alex, a girlfriend of mine from Brown also living in Fulham, and would soon go on to have a fling with Kelly. Nate had a gig in Camden the same evening so he could only stay an hour or so. We went into the kitchen where we had a rather stilted conversation.

'Thanks for coming, it's right the other side of London for you.' He was living around Bounds Green in a house share with four friends from his childhood in Ipswich, Suffolk.

'I really wanted to see you again.' I was uncomfortable with this purposeful declaration.

'Shame you missed the video of us all making fools of ourselves. Except you, of course. Shh, I don't want the others to hear me dissing their work.'

'You're the one that stands out.' Too much.

'Let me get you some food. You could do with feeding up.'

'Sorry Clea, but it won't make any difference. Believe me, I've tried to beef up. I might as well warn you now, I'm quite… thin.'

'Lucky you! You don't have to rely on crystal meth to stay looking good then, like me!'

'What's crystal meth, never heard of that? Some kind of speed I'm guessing.'

'Yeah. It's not over here yet. I heard about it in LA when I lived there.' I decided it was better to play it straight and not scare him off.

'I was thinking… I… might… try… and come back… after my gig. Is-that—alright?' It took him ages to spit out what he wanted to say and I felt the stirrings of his hesitation. We went into the drawing room where everyone was getting progressively drunker. I had a warm feeling inside generated by Nate's interest and this buoyed me.

The week before I had got on the telephone and invited friends I had not seen in a while, in some cases years. I was surprised when aloof Julian showed up at my door. He had been so scathing about my Sloaney friends while staying at their house in Cannes! We stood off from the now boisterous crowd peopling my living room, stairs and kitchen. We sat on the piano stool by the French windows that were open as no one was feeling the cold, and smoking was rife. Maybe because I had held back from Nate about my time in LA, I felt no such inclination with Julian. After I'd described my rocky descent into crystal meth addiction in LA, Julian put his hand under my chin, in a brotherly way.

'Well, I would say you really have succeeded in escaping your upbringing, Clea. No house in the country with a Volvo and 2.4 children for you.'

I was secretly delighted. 'We're all a bit young for that aren't we?'

'Actually no we're not.'

'I suppose. I just don't mix with that kind anymore.' We surveyed the vivacious, drunk and arty guests huddled in groups or jigging to the stereo.

'Yes, you're quite the chameleon, aren't you?'

'I'll take that as a compliment.'

'Just an observation, Clea. I wouldn't read too much into it, only that it hasn't gone unnoticed that you seem to be leading a life I never could have seen you leading a few years ago. A total reinvention.'

Always someone determined to remain on the periphery, Julian left soon after our chat to go on to another Christmas party. I now felt doubly buoyed, as I interpreted our conversation as one of admiration, but looking back I am not sure that was quite what he meant.

A man of his word, Nate reappeared around midnight when most of us had started dancing badly to 70s disco, knocking over the Christmas tree as well as a few drinks. He did not stay long as he needed to take the night bus home, but long enough for us to share a kiss in the corner, hidden by my grandmother's baby Grand. Days later I received a beautiful greetings card from him with a heartfelt message. The card was of a group of children playing outside in the snow and I was touched by its sensitivity and his sweet words. He was proving a gentleman.

Nate invited me to a gig at Up the Creek in Greenwich and we had a good time at the private party afterwards, all his attention on me. Sometimes when out, we drank copious amounts of alcohol. However, his personality did not change, whereas mine did. All the unresolved issues and traumas would come unstuck, surface, and oftentimes spew out at whoever was in my path. I could sometimes control myself, but I was an emotional time bomb. I was getting professional help, but my deep-seated self-hatred was still running the internal show.

I was also not entirely convinced I was properly attracted to Nate. I was flip-flopping. Inevitably I knew it would cause problems because after the first few times we made love, I lost interest. Not in him as a person and friend, but as a lover. He took this badly and my response was to drink too much, stagger into his bed before him, roll over and pretend to be asleep. Because he did not have that much experience with women, he did not challenge me.

It's relevant to mention my libido was not strong, or something I even thought about much, then. After the assault incident with Conrad in LA, and my subsequent arrest and unofficial deportation home to the UK, I was too 'full up' with unresolved baggage; sex was a burden, or an obligation more than anything. I also felt I had to preserve whatever external shell I held in place; I was hiding myself, even though I had no idea who that self was.

I enjoyed time with Nate, outside the bedroom. We would do quiet things like watch films, theatre, go for

163

walks and coffee. Neither of us had money and he liked it to be 'just the two of us'. When I was with him, I felt vaguely wrong-footed being the more dynamic one. By then I had revealed more of myself than I was comfortable with.

He'd also misplaced me on a pedestal. He was often saying, 'you're clearly out of my league'. I was usually attracted to men who made me work for their attention, but it was different with Nate and it did not bring out the best in me. Being such an emotion-based woman—or a victim at the mercy of my turbulent emotions—the reality that I did not get unduly excited about seeing Nate when we had been apart a while undermined my feelings for him, although I was also a coward who liked being able to say I had a boyfriend. It helped me feel validated and loved.

Writing about this time in my life is hard. My memories are hazy. I was so confused, due to the aftermath of crystal meth in LA and the toxicity still within my physical, mental and spiritual systems. Because the follow-up care had been almost non-existent after I'd left the Gordon Hospital, I was pretending I was normal: just like any other young woman in her mid-20s, trying to catch a break as a fledgling actress. But there was a heap of dysfunction barely beneath the surface.

For Valentine's Day, Nate invited me to his house for a meal. I knew he would make it special; he was extremely romantic, and liked experimenting in the kitchen. No effort was too much. However, even knowing this, I didn't arrive till midnight. And I had no good reason.

My father had suggested we go for an early evening drink at the Hurlingham Club, and I had agreed. 'A quick one'. My dad loved his clubs. While I drank wine and chatted, messages came through on the Motorola beeper Nate had bought me.

'Is everything okay? Our dinner is nearly ready. Can't wait to see you darling!'

I went to a payphone off the bar to call him, telling him I was at the club but would leave shortly. Well, I didn't. And not because I was having such a great time. Looking back, it is obvious I was not happy about the state of things and should have ended it. Eventually I rolled up at his house, worse for wear having got his last message 2 hours earlier: 'the food is not looking so good now.' I suppose it had vaguely tickled some notion of conscience within me. I stumbled through the front door nearly knocking him over and rolled down the corridor to the kitchen where a couple of his housemates sat at the table; I sobered quickly because you could cut the tension with a knife.

Nate might really like me, or even be in love with me, but his friends were unimpressed. They gave me the third degree about my whereabouts, and then harrumphed off in what I rightly perceived as fuzzy disgust. Nate had cooked an amazing spread that included wood pigeon and all sorts of delicate vegetables, artichokes and beetroot, cut into heart shapes of varying sizes and arranged beautifully. I'd never felt less deserving of someone's thoughtfulness!

As well as live performance, Nate was a talented artist, with a skill in draughtsmanship and everything he did, including cookery, meant he made it visually artistic and unique. This was not lost on me and I felt genuinely guilty, but not enough to mend my ways.

'Sorry my darling, but there's hardly any wine left.'

'Good thing I bought something with me then!' I pulled out a bottle I'd bought on my way over, even though I'd been running about four hours late. My excessive drinking was another unacknowledged elephant in the room. It almost felt like part of me was pushing him to see how far I could go, before he snapped.

'So what happened this evening?' Nate glanced at me sheepishly.

'You know my Dad and I have a tricky relationship—well, he was really opening up to me and I didn't want to cut that short because it doesn't happen often.'

I noticed he had a slight smile now like he got what I am talking about. My dad does not ever open-up, but I had to come up with something half viable. In fact, my dad and I had a wonderful relationship overall, in that he enabled me to be who I wanted. He rarely challenged me about anything, even when he could or should have. He accepted me unconditionally.

'That's good I guess, for you and him, I mean.' Nate graciously responded.

'Sorry! I know—not good for you though. I feel terrible. I know your friends hate me—I almost drowned in their dark looks when I walked in.'

'They're just looking out for me, Clea. They've been my best friends a long time, since I was eleven.'

'I know! Well, they won't last. You might all be playing happy families now but trust me, the friendships won't last.'

Nate looked upset by my outburst. Leaning in, I put my hand on his shoulder. 'Oh, come on, Nate, look. I don't know what I'm talking about. Just because mine didn't last doesn't mean it will be the same for you!'

'You mean you're a spoiled little rich girl.'

'What is that supposed to mean?'

'You tell me?'

'Well number one, how am I rich? That's ridiculous.'

'Boarding schools, rich friends, fancy houses, holidays, drinks at the Hurlingham.'

'Most of my friends these days aren't like that.'

'Well, if you treat your friends how you just treated me tonight, I'm not surprised they didn't last.'

That told me. In that moment, I decided I had better make it up to him at least in the short term. After I wolfed down the dinner Nate had reheated in the oven, we went to bed and this time I did not roll over and pretend to be asleep.

Nate and I sat at a small round table at the BBC bar at Television House, having filmed his comedy act for a new six-part series. He had written me into his extended comedy act, with minimal dialogue as my part was a parody of the glamorous game show hosts of the 50s. We had already done a handful of gigs on the London comedy circuit over the previous six months.

I still had my full face of makeup, but was happily out of the tight plum red satin and sequinned evening gown I had been costumed in, playing his smiley and dumb assistant.

Nate looked relieved as he took a glug of his pint. 'Thank you Clea, you know that was really above and beyond the call of duty.'

'What are you talking about? It's good for me too!' Things had hardly been progressing for me on the acting front and although being a part of Nate's act was a periphery experience, at least I was part—okay a minuscule part—of a TV show.

'I like you being in my act—I always said I'd use you if the opportunity arose—and it did.'

'Even though we aren't a couple anymore?' Nate looked away from me, while I waved at the costume lady who'd entered the bar with her assistant, trying to cover up my awkwardness. I gathered my belongings.

'Hang on, you're not going?' Nate put his hand on my arm.

'Well, it is getting late.'

'Please wait a little bit longer. I'll get in drinks, okay.' There was an urgency in his tone I found weirdly compelling, like he had a big secret to divulge.

He came back with a bottle of champagne on ice.

'Wow. What are we celebrating?'

Nate shrugged, smiled enigmatically, and set the glasses down, poured and we toasted each other and the show. I was at least anticipating news because he'd been in meetings with important broadcasters and producers over the last few months.

'To us.' He clinked my glass yet again.

I mumbled slightly drunken assent.

'The thing is—I really think—we should get married.' I double took, not believing my ears.

'Very funny.'

'I'm serious. I think we'd be great together!' Nate enthused, looking me directly in the eye. I had an avalanche in my stomach. I poured myself more champagne, stalling. We had broken up four months ago. It had come to the point where my behaviour towards him was appalling: I was always late, often rude and moody.

No doubt under duress from his friends, and having reached the end of his tether, he wrote me a letter ending it. He was about to go off on a European tour and I had yet again failed to show when I'd promised I would for a big gig in Camden. Nate felt humiliated and all his friends despised me now.

'You can't really see us married, can you?' I laughed, assuming he was taking the piss.

'Actually yes, yes I can. I'm happy to look after the babies and you can go off and be fabulous, act, work, whatever.'

'Babies!'

'You know I love babies. I've always wanted a family, you know that.'

'I'm sorry Nate, but I'm just not cut out for all that.'

'Okay… I get it! You're surprised, but I have thought a lot about all this—'

'Really!'

'Yes. What I have realised is that I have enough love for both of us, Clea. I can promise you that.' Nate had a teary look. I gathered my things quickly.

'Oh no, please don't go. At least come back to mine tonight, please.'

'I'm really sorry. I am really happy you brought me in on your act, but I can't do this. I'm sorry. I'm not right for you. Deep down I know you know that.'

I gave him a quick peck on the cheek and headed for the exit. I dared not look back.

I felt like a bad person.

I will add that Nate went on to have a hugely successful career in international entertainment, and a happy family life, without me.

Chapter 13

Alfie

We are made wise not by the recollection of our past, but by the responsibility for our future.

George Bernard Shaw

It was late. I was upstairs prepping for bed when the door knocker went, hard and urgent. I wasn't expecting anyone so I ignored it, thinking they had the wrong house and would realise their mistake. Then a pebble hit my window, then another followed by another, impatience clearly gaining; I threw open the curtains and lifted the old window frame to see a forlorn Alfie at the gate, loaded with bags and a couple suitcases. What the hell?

Not believing my eyes, I raced downstairs and opened the door. Alfie, the craggily handsome, rusty-haired boy I had been seeing for a month, was stooped and dejected. He was eight years older than me and we'd met in an acting class. He had been living in a bedsit in Chiswick near where he'd attended drama school. His long hair stood up in front like he was slightly surprised, or in shock. He was even more enervated and nervy than usual.

'I had no choice. I had to leave! That guy I told you about, the paranoid schizophrenic who I am guessing is on parole, well he threatened to burn my hair off. He should either be in prison or locked up in a psyche ward.'

'Oh my god! Come in.'

Alfie had already regaled me with the horrors of the men living alongside him in the unkempt, mould-infested building, each tenant living in almost-closet spaces. The first time I'd gone there we both were drunk, having been out for a few drinks after the acting class—I'd been shocked by his set-up even though he had pre-warned me. Additionally, he'd been too forceful in his sexual advances. I'd become uncomfortable and rushed away. I knew I'd see him again and did, a couple weeks later at the Actors Centre where he performed the tail-between-his-legs part beautifully. He was on a housing list and adamant he would get the one-bedroom flat he believed he deserved. He knew how to work the benefits system and had no qualms doing so.

'I couldn't stay longer, I just couldn't.' He eyed me plaintively. 'That's the third time he's threatened me. I'm scared for my life, Clea! Really I am.'

'You told me about the first time when he pushed you down the stairs, but what happened the second time?' I wasn't quite buying his story.

'He pulled a knife on me. Luckily, he was so drunk and stoned he couldn't aim straight and I kicked him in the shins and the moron toppled.'

'Oh my god! Why didn't you tell me before?'

'I didn't want to make you nervous and then you wouldn't come over to see me anymore.'

'So, you've left the bedsit for good?' I looked at his belongings, touched he'd come to me.

'How can I stay there? The guy wants me dead!'

'Did you call the police?'

'Of course I bloody well did. Do you think I'm a moron, Clea? This guy, Phil the Pill, claims I made it all up. That he wouldn't hurt a fly because he's been rehabilitated. He says I'm crazy!'

Something I liked about Alfie—initially—was his enthusiasm. Wherever he was, there was drama. Often what attracted me would repel me by the end.

'I would have thought the police would have taken the side of a reasonable, well-spoken, polite, white, middle-class man like you rather than that fruit loop?'

'Oh, they don't care. It's more hassle than it's worth to them. It's dog-eat-dog in that fleapit building from hell.'

'So, it looks like you need a place to stay.' He leaned in and gave me a tender kiss. What I secretly believed was that he wanted to move in with me, but knew it was too early in our relationship. I'd have to be a horrible person to not let him stay, and Alfie had that way—gift of the gab—of inveigling himself into your good graces. 'Just a few nights' would end up being over a year.

'My little guardian angel,' he murmured in my ear while we lay spooning, right before I dropped off to sleep.

For all the drama that emanated around Alfie like a lingering, potent smell, he also had a kind side, along with his more obvious charms—chiselled good looks in the ilk of a Romany gypsy, a dark and rusty-haired mystery. He'd been brought up with a younger sister who'd been born with Downs syndrome and was teased mercilessly at school, before his parents had finally got her into a Special Needs school. He'd been her daily protector; this made him a fighter for the underdog. The only problem was that by the time we got together he perceived himself as the underdog, desperate to escape that position.

I also felt that he viewed me as damaged, which I was, and that I was playing a substitute role for his now deceased sister whose kidneys had failed in her early 20s.

I had been back from Los Angeles for four years and even though I'd had six months of psychotherapy we had not made progress, beyond me offloading and telling my story. Retrospectively I would say that this therapist had compassion, but not the other necessary insights to help me. I was using alcohol destructively—to cover my residual shame and unconscious self-hatred—and this bled into my relationships, chiefly the ones with men.

My tendency with Alfie was to get drunk and then physically attack him: I'd punch and kick him until I received a response. Only once did he hit back and that was near the end of our relationship; I'd been vile, taunting him all night, pushing him to the limit.

On one of our first dates, I spat at him in a fit of pique about him focusing more talk-time on his female friend, Tabitha, who he'd invited for a drink to meet me.

It had been clear there was no sexual chemistry between them, but part of me wanted a scene to prove I was important. I've since learned my need for negative attention is a conditioned behaviour. I can surmise that both she and Alfie knew there was something deeply wrong with me, and felt compassion.

Alfie later confided he'd found the spitting incident worse than all the other physical violence because it seemed a more intimate aggression. My way of getting attention, even if it was 'negative'; I perceived it as a show of love.

He always forgave me, but the situation was worsening because one day after work (I worked part-time as a receptionist for a law firm in South Kensington) my boss called me into his office and quietly closed the door behind me. He was a balding, cocky man who lived in a Surrey mansion and drove a Ferrari.

'Righty ho, Clea.' He looked at me, as if for inspiration. I thought perhaps he was going to fire me, but couldn't think why as my skill-set far outdid the requirements of my job.

'What is it, Gerald?' Now I detected a distinct whiff of embarrassment. Had he fallen madly and passionately in love with me? I doubted it although the idea tickled me.

'The thing is…' He sighed, then scratched the side of his bald head.

'Yes?' I prompted. He then loosely pointed at the bruises on my shins and upper arms. I had covered them up, or thought I had, but it had been a particularly humid, summer day and the foundation had rubbed off.

'The thing is… you don't and shouldn't have to put up with this kind of thing. You're a nice young lady and… well, it's not right, now, is it?' He looked relieved having vaguely articulated what was on his mind. Then I got it. He thought some horrible man was beating me up!

'It's not like that, Gerald! Really, it's not.' But how on earth was I to articulate how it was? Even to my own ears my strangulated tones sounded false. I didn't understand it myself, and there was clearly a problem, but it categorically was not my boyfriend Alfie. I was the cause! Alfie would literally hold me back from beating him up. (I would get to the bottom of my dysfunctions, but that would be in the future). Gerald stood behind his executive desk and looked directly at me, shaking his head in a resigned 'well I've tried' way.

I had to stop myself running out of his office back to the relative safety of the reception area. I was rather touched he'd taken the time to 'help' me, but this diminished soon after when again he called me into his office and told me I should give up the ridiculous idea of being an actress and do something 'proper'.

Having two thespians together was always going to be challenging. However, it fell to me to be the one that led the more structured daily life, working two part-time jobs, one in a bar and the other in an office making use of the facilities—printing and photocopying—for both of us. This was before the mass use of the internet and email, when actors needed a constant supply of headshots and CVs, while also writing formal, typed cover letters when applying for acting jobs.

Alfie was a contradiction, keeping up a reputation as a hell-raiser but obsessed with health and looks. Vanity was his Achilles' heel and later became his most unattractive trait.

When he brought himself a new Tom Ford black leather jacket for Christmas, rather than contributing cash for the payment of his son's guitar lessons, it gave me serious pause. I have my selfish moments, but his constant proclamation that he needed to look the 'star' to get lead parts was more than grating on my frayed nerves.

I was never in love with Alfie. We claimed to love the other, but mutual passion was not evident. Like attracts like. We both suffered from love starvation, but it manifested differently.

I quickly recognised his capacity for patience and tolerance, exemplified by our third date. We'd arranged to meet at Richmond Station and I was three hours late; mobile phones were in their infancy and I didn't have one, so there was no way to contact him. He waited, and met me with open arms.

At the last hour, the night before my mother had deigned to let me know my grannie's cremation was the next day in Brighton. I'd been regularly visiting my grannie in her Hove nursing home, so I knew she'd died, but it was up to my mother to make the arrangements. It was only my mother, stepfather, myself and a carer from the home at the service. I had not spoken to my mother for over a year. When we went to a restaurant for lunch in the Lanes afterwards, instigated by my stepfather, nothing was mentioned about the last time my mother and I had seen each other.

This distancing had come about after my 30th birthday when she'd visited the UK to see her best friend, Melanie, who also lived in Fulham. She'd ruined the evening just like she'd done on many occasions, including my 21st birthday and graduation, going into a silent rage aimed at my stepfather over dinner, and then at my graduation dinner she verbally annihilated my father in a fit of aggressive rage, accusing him of being a 'fucking loser' (a favoured catch-all phrase) in front of my college friends.

When the focus was not on her and her myriad needs, whether praise, adoration or attention of any kind, my mother ripped the scene to shreds; she possessed an uncanny ability for detecting a weak point. At my graduation, for example, my father got it as he'd pointedly spent as little time around her as possible. A narcissist with a few gins is a frightening sight, which was apparent in the miscomprehension and child-like hurt on my sweet father's face, when she leaned into his ear and stage whispered: 'You're a fucking loser, Bill Myers. You're a disgrace to your family!' I inwardly crumpled, believing I'd somehow made this happen.

I spent the rest of the week pushing down metaphorical vomit. I wished she'd never bothered to cross the Atlantic, but it was too late for that. Years later I'd understand the mechanics of narcissistic rage where my mother frequently felt easily slighted and unjustly treated, as if something she'd felt entitled to had been taken. Her own emptiness was reflected at her through others' lack of apparent empathy and mirroring; her husband Johnny usually supplied her fuel or 'supply', but he'd decided to skip my graduation out of respect for my father. Or rather that is what he claimed, but I think he relished the time away from mum.

My mother ended up spending most of her trip with the family of one of my housemates; they'd rented a limo that they took on day trips around Rhode Island. She worked her charm beautifully and they were much enamoured; she repaid them by taking only photographs of my friend walking the 'graduation walk' through Brown's historic gates, and ignored me. There was not one photograph of me—all of them were of my friend and her family!

This did not go unnoticed by my friend. If mummy was behaving in a non-embarrassing, or humiliating fashion I put up with her. After all, she was my mother and I loved her. Sometimes her gaze would land favourably on me, and it was those moments I was still holding out for. Occasionally we'd have a good day out: lunch and shopping. The moments she'd say, 'you're not so bad, after all!'

My thirtieth birthday was another marker in the bumpy ride of my destructive relationship with my mother. This birthday was painful because the evening had started well and ended so disastrously. Over the make-up telephone call, we'd even promised each other it would be a success, but then she'd had that one drink too many. My good friend Louise from Heathfield was renting the spare room in our house and joined us for dinner. We walked to Melanie and Phil's house, near the Hurlingham Club, where we sat in the drawing room and drank champagne. My mother raised her hands dramatically, demanding the small gathering quietened.

'Clee, my lovely daughter, here is your birthday present!' She raised her hands to the back of her neck and undid the clasp to her favourite pearls, given to her by her errant father for her 21st. She'd worn them every day for almost 40 years. I could not believe my eyes. I don't actually like pearls—they remind me of powdery old ladies—but I was bowled over by her heartfelt gesture. Louise, a non-drinker, sipped her usual Coke and admired them, while my mother made a dramatic moment of placing them round my neck. When my mother shined her light on me it felt so good, like I was suspended in a big flash of warmth and light. We all cheered each other with a toast to me, champagne flutes refilled by Phil who knew better than to leave my mother's glass empty, while Melanie joked that I'd better insure the pearls as I was hardly the most responsible of people. Considering I secretly knew I'd pawned any valuable jewellery I'd had in

LA, what hadn't been stolen, she wasn't that far off.

So far so good.

We left for a local Italian restaurant on Fulham Road. We ordered food while wine flowed. At some point between the starter and the main the atmosphere changed, subtly but noticeably. My mother had already had a dig at me about my burgeoning acting career. I was in rehearsals for a profit-share musical play, *Cold Comfort Farm*, based on the novel by Stella Gibbons. I'd already explained the financial mechanics of what constituted profit share, but my mother decided to expand this conversation.

Sipping her wine—she prided herself on being a slow sipper—she looked directly at me. 'Well, Clee, such a shame you had to leave LA. Now you are reduced to… community plays. Hardly glamorous darling, is it?'

'No, it's not glamorous at all, but the point is I'm learning an awful lot. And who knows where it might lead.' I doubt my mother had ever attended a London Fringe theatre play in her life.

I was unfazed. The reality was I had no formal drama training so this was where I'd learn my craft, as well as ad hoc classes in movement, voice, Meisner and Strasberg techniques. She'd never been interested in details, just proclamations; I recalled she'd written in my childhood autograph book: 'I can't wait to see your name up in lights one day'. That was really what she wanted for herself, but she'd never pursued anything long enough. It pained her on some deep, if never acknowledged level. The closest she'd got was becoming a BBC World Service newsreader in Dubai when I was in my early teens. Posted there with my stepfather who worked in the oil business, she'd loved the 4am starts, editing the news source and quickly learning the multi-syllabled names of the various Emirate Sheiks. But her marriage went on the rocks and her husband forced her to return to the UK; that was the end of her broadcasting career, even though she'd been very good and even received fan mail.

'I think it's wonderful Clea is giving the acting a go. It takes courage at her age,' Melanie said, kindly.

'Well, I just love it so much! If you can make a living doing what you love, surely that's an incredible goal—'

'Oh, what do you know about making a living?' my mother side hissed at me; Louise quickly caught my eye in warning: *don't let her get under your skin*.

'I do have a couple side jobs, Mum. I'm busy all the hours of the day!'

'Pah! And to think all that money that was spent on your expensive education.'

'Well, who knows. Maybe it will all hold me in good stead. There is, after all, always value to be had from a good education.'

'I wouldn't know!' Mummy knocked back her drink, with a touch of defiance.

'Well, I remember being the head secretary in my typing pool and I couldn't wait to get out of there, start a family,' Melanie said.

'Well, you married the boss. Of all the most unoriginal things to do! But then you've always been a coward and played it safe.'

Melanie and I exchanged a look; we'd both been here before.

I jumped at the sound of Phil's chair scraping back on the tiles.

'Righty-ho. I think I'll be off now. Lovely to see you, Clea. Happy birthday.'

'Where's he going?' Mummy pierced his receding back with her big hazel eyes.

'He did mention earlier he needed to get off early to finish his editing on the *Hurlingham Newsletter*. He wasn't going to come, but you changed his mind.'

'How could anyone resist you, Mummy.' I smiled encouragingly, although my sixth sense told me where we were headed.

'We don't need your sarcasm, Clea.'

We all ignored that, but the energy had shifted and we were back to the familiar walking on eggshells that was my childhood. Louise got up to go to the loo, looking like she too would rather be walking out the restaurant. I refilled our glasses with the fresh bottle of Sancerre; the waiter had not returned. This was another area where my mother had created difficulties in the past.

'You should not be doing that! That's the waiter's job!' she exclaimed resentfully, flinging a black look over at the waiter who was too busy clearing a table to notice. I clocked that she was happy for me to fill up her empty glass before expressing her dissatisfaction. She'd made a scene at a posh Indian in South Kensington once when the older European waitress did not return her smile, making snide comments while she took our orders; I was mortified, but her friends ignored her as if they were dealing with an unruly child.

'It's a hard job being a waitress. Or a barman. People can be very impatient and treat you like a machine, or a robot.'

'Like I don't know? I was cleaning and scrubbing pub

floors if you remember, Clea, while you swanned off to the Caribbean.' She was referring to the time when she was separated from my stepfather and he'd got behind on her monthly alimony. She'd panicked and got the first job she could find in a local pub. She'd worked there a few nights for three weeks.

'Well, you didn't last there long, now did you?' Melanie joked. I knew this was a mistake.

'What do you know about anything? All you've ever done is marry the first man that asked you and live off him like a limpet. Not to mention the appalling social climbing you both thrive on. If it wasn't for Bill and I, you'd have never have got near the Hurlingham Club, let alone become members.' Her vitriol was palpable. Melanie looked off into the distance.

'Shall we have dessert?' she suggested to Louise and I.

'I've lost my appetite,' I said.

'No, I'm fine thanks,' Louise almost whispered.

And then my big mistake followed.

'I can't believe you'd speak to your best friend like that, Mummy. I mean it's just such a horrible thing to say.' I paused, naively thinking she might agree and quickly apologise so we could rewind to the perfectly pleasant evening we'd been enjoying.

'How dare you,' she hissed. 'Who do you think you are, Clea Myers? You are nothing! A spoiled brat and a total fuck up. A loser. I'm ashamed that you're my daughter.'

Melanie and Louise looked dumbstruck. The bill arrived and my mother grabbed it, flinging down a credit card while the waiter rushed it through, as we were rather making a scene.

'Go home! I can't bear the sight of you.'

'Come on!' Louise put her arm through mine and whispered that we'd be better off leaving. I felt so confused with my slight drunkenness and wondering what the hell had happened.

'But it's my birthday—I don't want it to end like this!' The sickeningly familiar gaping space within me had expanded. Mummy had already exited and was striding down the road, Melanie a couple steps behind, trying to keep up. Mummy always got an incredible surge of energy through her fits of pique. I called after her, but she ignored me.

When I got home, I tried calling to patch it up. Melanie answered and Mummy refused to speak to me. The same happened the next day and then the next. I was devastated. To feel her glow of approval and have it so quickly ripped away was excruciating.

My feelings of abandonment manifested as depression and desperation for love. Love starvation! My mother and I did not speak for another year and a half, when my stepfather made the initial call about Grannie's cremation. Naturally my birthday was never referred to, as per usual, like it had not happened. Problems were deemed the usual mother-daughter rumblings.

However, no one I knew had a similar situation with their mother, and this contributed to my shame and isolation. I believed deep down that there was something very, very wrong with me.

Alfie proved a balm. He was focused—on himself primarily—but certain lifestyle aspects bled into mine— yoga, healthy eating and fitness.

Then his father died, leaving his mother a lonely

widow. We'd spent quite a few weekends with them in their cottage in Swanage, Dorset, where Alfie's son lived with Alfie's ex-partner. His son did not take to me; he saw me as an interloper and a robber of his father's time.

I think Alfie's dad's death exacerbated whatever it was within himself that needed healing; he also lost interest in sex. I was not particularly bothered, but he was. We'd fight often.

Most fights were about what I perceived as his attitude. He could be incredibly kind, and a real advocate for the underdog, but he could be selfish too. When my dad and I sold up our house in Fulham, where we all lived, it was left to me to pack. Alfie disappeared and did not ever help me clear or pack even one box. The move was tough. Alfie never paid rent either, although he contributed to bills.

This was the terrace house in Parsons Green, in Fulham, where I'd witnessed my father deteriorate throughout my childhood, after my mum left him. He'd descended into a depression; he'd changed nothing and her aura still permeated the walls. Everything had fallen into disrepair, reflected in my dad's sombre ways. I'd never felt good living in that place. A dank cloud hung over me there.

When I started the process of packing, I felt like my dad shirked the responsibility onto me. He never dealt with his feelings. I found all sorts of my mother's remnants, including the file called 'Operation Eagle'. As mentioned earlier my mother had been disinherited by her wealthy father just after I was born. She had been led to mistakenly believe, by her mother, that she stood to inherit his fortune, but he disinherited my mum in favour of his nephew. I think this traumatic event lead her into the arms of my flashy stepdad, because as she later remarked, my father had not 'backed her up'. Perhaps an act of revenge stemming from so much loss and hurt.

This file contained all sorts of legal documents, although I quickly surmised my mother hadn't a chance of winning any legal inheritance battle. She had never shared this with me.

Part of my resentment towards Alfie was the divide between his public and private persona: all smiles for the world out there, while I had an insecure big baby on my hands. After his father died unexpectedly of a heart attack, I had been as supportive as I could, helping him organise the funeral, typing and printing the order of service, generally being a decent and kind girlfriend. Alfie had excelled in his organisation and running of the service; he read Keats, whom his father had loved, and played selected songs by the classical singer, Kathleen Ferrier.

The funeral was also the third time I met his son. I'd had a hard time believing Alfie had a son because his life contradicted anything suggesting stability—unresolved debts, an uncertain career trajectory, no material assets. His son was eleven and called Joseph, or Joe. Joe's mum was pleasant enough and ten years older than Alfie; she didn't hold residual anger towards him even though we all knew he hadn't behaved brilliantly, although she did mutter at the tea and biscuits following the service, when he'd mislaid his mobile phone, 'he's always been useless.'

It was hard picturing Alfie and her together. Joe wasn't interested in me at all and ran off the first time we met, back to his mother. Alfie consoled me that it was par for the course, even though I'd bought him a present—*World of Warcraft* as suggested by Alfie—and taken him out for a cream tea in a local café. It was all new ground, uncomfortable territory. A consolation was the fact that Alfie found the part time responsibility of one child enough, so having children would never be an issue between us. Motherhood made something inside me silently scream.

One morning after another unpleasant encounter between me and Alfie, started by my annoyance at the length of time he spent in the house's only bathroom, he suggested we attend Relate to save our relationship. Since college, I was a believer in counselling and therapy, so I was surprised but pleased he suggested this. More than anything I saw it as proof he loved me, although his behaviour belied this. Alfie persuaded me we had something worth saving. I wasn't fully convinced as I didn't believe it should be so much hard work, so early on.

I arrived first at the Relate offices on Tottenham Court Road. Alfie sauntered in a few minutes later, with his casual sloping walk and cool demeanour, undoubtedly making the pretty young woman at the reception desk feel special with his smile zoom-focused on her. When he noticed me already sitting there, filling in the paperwork, he waved hesitantly like he was embarrassed I'd witnessed his smooth entrance. Shame he didn't bother to turn on the Alfie charm for me anymore.

A woman with slightly greying, brown cropped hair approached us, introducing herself as Anthea. She ushered us into a room with two small sofas and a coffee table in the middle. We all settled and she gave us an inquisitive look, waiting for one of us to break the silence.

'Right. Well as this was my idea, I'll start,' Alfie offered.

'Great. Go ahead Alfie,' Anthea quietly prompted.

'Okay. Clea has a lot of problems and I think she's projecting onto me most of the time.'

'What sort of problems, in your opinion?'

'Well. Clea can be very aggressive. There have been quite a few occasions when she's attacked me for no apparent reason. And worst of all for me, as an actor, she scratched my face.' He angled his face toward Anthea. 'And it could have stopped me getting the job. And it was my first audition for a West End play. It was like she was deliberately trying to sabotage me.'

I looked at him and thought *you know that isn't true, at least the sabotage part*, but hearing him describe it out loud made my skin crawl with a familiar shame. I really wanted to leave and ideally never see Alfie again. Anthea looked at me, and to my surprise gave me an encouraging smile. I guess I was waiting for her to annihilate me, like my mother would with the usual accusations: you're a loser with a capital L, hideously selfish, unnecessarily cruel.

'Alcohol definitely doesn't bring the best out in me. That's why I've knocked it on the head. But now according to Alfie, I've become boring.'

'No. It's just that it wasn't always bad, you know, not always consistently bad. We had fun times too, like at Carnival last year in Notting Hill. Other times too, like when we stayed at the Mermaid hotel in Rye. We had a few special days together there over the Millennium.'

I recall how we'd been involved with each other at Carnival the previous year even though we were surrounded by his friends, when he'd been willing to shine his light on me. It hadn't lasted.

'All of which I paid for,' I stated matter-of-factly, as if I was fine about it.

'You were the one insistent that we go away together like a,' he raised his hands to make air quotes, 'normal couple.'

'No fear of anyone mistaking us for that, Alfie.' I attempted a laugh that sounded hollow even to me.

'I'm sensing undercurrents of hostility between you. I think I should ask the question: what is it that either of you hope to gain from these sessions? We have eight scheduled and although that might sound like a lot, believe me, they pass quickly.'

'I would like to establish genuine communication,' I said succinctly.

'Alfie?'

'Errrm, yeah, me too. Though I think we communicate okay, on the whole.'

'Then what the hell are we sitting here for?' I shot back at him. I noticed Anthea's impassive face and a sense of foreboding, mingled with extreme tiredness, hit me. Was there any point to all this? My confidence in Anthea's abilities had dwindled; I think she needed to be more authoritative, less free-wheeling.

'Okay so let's start with the other night,' I proffered.

Alfie slightly raised his eyebrows like he'd heard it all before.

'Go on Clea.' Anthea gestured a small, sweeping action and I noticed she was not wearing a wedding or indeed an engagement ring.

'Are you married then?' I asked her, noticing the note

of petulance in my voice.

'Divorced actually.' She gave me a thin-lipped smile.

'How is that relevant, Clea? And it's rude!' Alfie admonished me.

'Well, you'd certainly know about that. As I was saying before I went so rudely off-track, we were out at a night club the other night in the west end. We were with our actor friend Adam—'

'Who hangs on everything she says!' Alfie interrupted jokily.

'At least he bloody well listens to me! Shut up, Alfie, you'll get your go… where was I? So, we are sitting in this corner that has a built-in seating arrangement and the three of us are happily drinking and chatting away. Then this group of tourists arrive—'

'They weren't tourists, they all lived and worked in London,' Alfie interjected, while Anthea raised her hand gently to shush him.

'Well, you would know! Basically, Alfie spent the rest of the evening speaking to them. For hours. He ignored me from then on. Wouldn't even dance with me once, not even to one of my favourite songs. And Adam noticed. I asked him afterwards if he thought I was overreacting. It was like you had to prove you were the most interesting person in the whole bloody place. But my main complaint is that you disrespected me. The three women were flabbergasted when I eventually spoke to them and told them you were my boyfriend, who lived with me; one of them was banking on going home with you.'

'Bollocks! Oops sorry,' he looked at Anthea apologetically, 'but I was just enjoying chatting with them, I wasn't "chatting" anyone up.'

'Saying it out loud just makes me sound so ridiculously petty, but that kind of stuff happens all the time.'

Silence.

Anthea indicated I should continue, while Alfie looked daggers at me.

'Ridiculous.' Alfie shook his head and looked off.

'Okay, here's another example. We'd arrange to meet outside a theatre to see a play and Alfie went round greeting everyone else, like his long lost best friends, and he wouldn't even acknowledge me. His reasoning being he'd already seen me in the morning. If you didn't know we were together, you'd think he was a totally free agent.'

'Why do you do that, Alfie? I can see how that could be interpreted as disrespectful to Clea.' I could see Alfie was about to lurch into his justification, but I was on a roll now, and stopped him.

'He has a philosophy about "sheeple" and following the crowd, or rather in our case not following the crowd. To him that's all just bourgeois crap—being polite and following the societal norms. Which, okay, to start with I thought sounded cool, but with all his "networking" he is so obsessed with, he certainly seems to be following exceptionally "normal" codes of conduct. Rather bourgeois I'd even hazard to call him!'

Alfie looked like an unhappy rabbit in headlamps. Had I betrayed him, I wondered for a few seconds, but then felt my bile rising again. 'Oh yeah. And I am working two jobs at the moment and on a Friday night I come home and want to play my stereo loud and I don't know—maybe act like a young person—and old man Alfie's having none of it because he's got some new regime—what's the latest fad?—Chinese medicine I believe, and he needs to be in bed by 10pm.'

'It didn't stop you from staying up all night blaring bloody Queen.' He attempted to sing a few bars of 'I Want to Break Free'.

Alfie and I stumbled on. He'd decided to make a dent in the VO (voice-over) acting world. He knew he had an excellent voice. I thought it was a good idea and he would regularly attend networking events.

He'd gone out to an event on a Friday night. I had been working at the bar/café at the Bridge Club some Fridays. I'd come home hoping to open a bottle of red with him, but he was nowhere to be seen so I went to bed early instead.

The next morning, he was still not home. This had never happened before. By 2pm I was worried. I'd left messages on his mobile, but it went to voicemail. I met up with a girlfriend to distract myself, and we saw a film.

I got home around 8pm. Fifteen minutes later, Alfie arrived back.

I was now angry.

'Where have you been?'

'Come here, come here. Gimme a cuddle!'

'Are you joking me! You've been gone over 24 hours! I was about to go to the police.'

'Okay I'll explain.'

'You better!'

'I went to the party at that hotel on Tottenham Court Road. Loads of free booze. Well, I hadn't eaten and I ended up getting arrested.'

'What?' It's not adding up.

'Yeah! For being drunk and disorderly. I was with Max;

you know how nuts he can be.' Max was a handsome actor friend of Alfie's who generally sleazed around.

'I thought you were supposed to be networking—'

Alfie grabbed both my hands, kissing them: 'Marry me!'

'What?' I was caught off guard.

'I love you! Marry me.'

'Whoa!' I had nothing more to say.

I left for a walk in the dark because I was so angry. I was also sick of fighting. I knew the proposal was a diversion tactic. He'd spent the night with another woman, I was convinced.

We had three counselling sessions left. Alfie had not made the last one, and it looked like he was not going to make this one. I'd stopped making excuses for him now to Anthea.

I'd shared with Anthea that I was about to start rehearsing a restoration play and how excited I was about that. I was to play Madame Marwood in Congreve's *The Way of the World*. It was a fringe production showing at The Starting Gate in North London, but I was thrilled nonetheless.

I had grown to like Anthea and her straightforward counsel. Both Alfie and I had spoken of our childhoods, but by this point Alfie was looking for a one-on-one psychoanalyst. Part of me suspected he did not rate Anthea. She was not shy to challenge him, but he always found wriggle room to justify himself.

'As this is Couple Counselling, I can't really work with just you, Clea.'

'I know.'

'I shouldn't really say this, but—'

'What?'

'This is not really appropriate, but in this case, I'm going to say it anyway.'

'Please do!'

'The best thing you can do for yourself Clea, is end this relationship.'

Somehow, I knew that was what she was going to say. She also said I had unresolved childhood trauma and needed to seek help for that. I was not convinced, but was grateful for her honesty and compassion.

Neither Alfie nor I attended the last session with Anthea. He had a call-back, and I had secretly given up on us. Then he was assigned the flat he'd been waiting for on the housing list, and promptly moved out while I was planning my own move from Fulham to Pimlico.

By this point he'd got a prescription for Viagra. We decided to meet at my new place for dinner. I especially wanted him to look at my new showreel, which I'd recently had edited.

Alfie arrived, excited. He had a call back for a TV job—a new police series—and he had Viagra in his back pocket. My plan was for us to watch my new showreel before we ate, but that time was eaten up by Alfie's exuberance and excitement at the call back. Fair enough.

We ate, chatted more and he declared himself exhausted. I brought up watching my showreel again, but all he said was, 'let's do that next week.'

He never watched my showreel.

We limped on for a couple more months, then I called it quits.

Alfie sobbed dramatically, but he started dating a

young dancer three months later so I can only assume he was not too heartbroken.

Chapter 14

Edward, the Tory

What happens is not as important as how you react to what happens.

Ellen Glasgow

I met Edward through an older male friend who worked in publishing. Paul lived in a large Victorian house in Brixton where he regularly threw parties, celebrating Halloween or Guy Fawkes, alongside birthdays. I had noticed Edward once before at a party, but mainly for being on the short side, which is rather unfair as he was 5'10".

He had the kind of face that always looked young and mischievous, with alert blue eyes and pale, freckled fine skin. Almost on meeting and starting to chat we lurched into mutual diatribes about what we perceived as our parents' failings, in my case my mother and for him, his errant father. He was a type I had deliberately sidestepped for years—ex-public school. I had immersed myself with creatives, actors mainly, but after Alfie I was doing my usual reactionary thing: tried that, didn't work, so let's swing back to something familiar, at least in terms of social background.

Sipping Bucks Fizz, I tentatively looked around the

traditional, book-stuffed study to clock if anyone was smoking. To my surprise Edward appeared at my side, his round, amiable face lit with a cheeky smile. He produced a crumpled pack of Camels from his jeans back pocket.

'I know that look of desperation! We can be the naughty kids in the corner together.'

'Camels are a bit strong. But thanks, they'll do.'

'Beggars can't really be choosers, can they?' He winked at me.

'Indeed.'

'Are you, by any chance, high maintenance, Clea?'

'Definitely not! I have been told I am pretty easy going.'

'Are you sure? Are you really, really sure about that?' I couldn't help but notice his weak chin while he teased me. He was not up there with the best lookers I'd previously stepped out with but still, I felt an attraction.

'I think I'm fairly easy going, at least that's what I've been told.' I was hardly going to share that my last relationship had ended with unsuccessful couples counselling. 'Well, of course the exception to that rule would be my mother, who doesn't have anything positive to say.'

'How often do you see the old dragon then?' This jarred; it was okay for me to criticise her, but he'd triggered my conditioned protectiveness.

'I haven't been to see her in France for over three years now. The last time we had a huge row. She was screaming at me how I was "a fucking loser". Oh yeah, and then I locked her out of her own house. Well, you can imagine how well that went down.'

Edward nodded conspiratorially. 'She does sound

rather like a genuine nut job. I haven't seen my dad for almost eight years.'

'Doesn't help that she lives in an awkward place to get to. Basically, the middle of rural South West France. Fine for a holiday but why they chose to live there I have no idea.'

'My dad lives in Portugal. Alongside his new ready-made family. Oh yes, he also had problems with the UK Medical Board.'

'So he's a doctor?'

'A surgeon, heart's his speciality. Ironic considering he doesn't appear to have one. That's how he met my mum— she was a nurse. She makes up for him. She is one amazing lady.'

There is nothing more appealing than a man who speaks lovingly and kindly of his mother, although I would come to question this later. He divulged more unsavoury details about his dishonest and unsavoury father and I knew we had established a bond, when he offered to drive me home. Trauma bonding, but I was not aware of this then. We'd huddled together the last couple of hours, while everyone else mingled around us. I found that initial easy rapport seductive, like we were lost souls finding each other. My hope was that maybe, just maybe, we would fix each other.

Later Edward confessed he'd always known we would end up together after we'd met, but he certainly played his cards close to his chest, initially. He lived in Victoria, literally up the road from me in Pimlico and from what I could gather was working himself up the greasy political pole within the Conservative Party. I had not reacted well when I first heard his political affiliation, being of the liberal left, but he made a convincing case for the Tories. He was also an advocate of Game Theory, which he applied to dating. Hence, after our first proper date in a Thai Restaurant he walked me home, kissed me quickly on my doorstop and then unceremoniously left. Our second date was a fresh afternoon stroll and coffee in Battersea Park where we flirtatiously skirted round each other. Our third was his invitation to join him at a Tory Fundraiser. If his plan (what he referred to as Game Theory) was to hook me, it worked. My usual approach of jumping straight in, head first, had been rumbled and he'd intuited that his slow(er), more gentlemanly approach would get me good and proper.

The night of the Fundraiser we met in a pub near the venue, and he made suitably impressed noises at my efforts. Having become so looks-obsessed when I lived in LA I was more relaxed back in London, living in my uniform of designer jeans, a mix of similar tops and a variety of splendid boots. I'd intuited Edward appreciated a girly style, so eager to please I dressed accordingly in a beige strapless and fake fur-trimmed sheaf dress, probably the most flattering I have owned. And I had straightened my wispy blonde hair to achieve a sleek look that clearly went down well with him.

He whispered, 'I think we'll be attending more fundraisers from now on.'

So far, so good. Off we went to the buffet dinner and he introduced me to a slew of polite, congenial people with whom we all made social chitchat. I noticed Edward was not interested in eating at all, but was liberally buying bottles of wine from the bar and generously sharing it out as well as slurping it down himself. This party girl had no problem with that—after all, it was a party, and the best tend to be drunken ones where people lose their inhibitions. Still, there was a shift in him, which would come back to haunt me.

He also got on better with women than men, which I took as a good sign, especially as most of them were older and less glamorous than me, but I suspected this could activate my green-eyed monster.

He wasn't keen to stay till the end and nor was I; we had yet to spend the night together, although the sexual tension had been building over our slew of dates. He was set on controlling the outcome and they always ended on a kiss at my front door. We took a taxi back to his flat and he got excited about a DVD he wanted to show me. About Kite surfing! I surveyed the maroon and magnolia decor of his living room alongside the Monet prints, inwardly digesting his unsophisticated and artless taste; certainly, no bohemian.

I sat on the velvet maroon sofa, leaned back in what I hoped looked a seductive pose and resigned myself to the show. And it was a show with his running commentary as these professional surfers rode the wind and waves. I was in the early throes of falling in love so I found him endearing and it all seemed vaguely amusing—and passion is always attractive—but I was confused why he was slurring his words. In between his wonky commentary, 'whoa watch him catch that huge one' and 'phoarrrr there goes another blinder', interspersed with cascading watery sound effects, he kept disappearing to his kitchen to refill his glass with what I assumed was orange juice. After about an hour, out of curiosity, I snuck up behind him, a half minute after he'd left me languishing on the sofa pretending to be interested in bloody kite surfing, and saw him shove a large vodka bottle back in the cupboard.

'I don't believe it. All this time I thought you were drinking orange juice and you've been on the vodka!' I was equally annoyed and bemused, partly because vodka would have alleviated the intense boredom I had managed to hide watching the interminable kite-surfing DVD and tickled because it was audacious.

'I-I-I didn't think you'd want any!' He reddened and avoided eye contact.

'Well, the polite thing to do would have been to ask, right?' I cajoled. I saw instantaneously his relief that I was not going to judge or admonish him.

'Of course, you can have some… or rather how about I mix us my speciality, a Caipirinha.' He grabbed fresh tumblers off the shelf and rustled through his cupboards for ingredients.

'Marvellous! I think I will join you then.' And there was my first mistake: joining him in the drink's stakes. Not that I would ever keep up, but I tried. And here my 'if only…' came into play. If only I had accepted what he was, realised I would never change him and left… But no, I had to stay for the ride.

'You're amazing Edward, you really are. Really kind.' Louise flicked her shiny, deep brown hair back, bestowing Edward her most gracious, wide smile while I internally smiled because I had heard this sob story a few times now. I recalled when he first shared with me his family situation about a month after we got together. He'd been anxious, as if I might perceive it as a black mark against him. In fact, it served the opposite and he had been bringing it out as a perverse party piece ever since, and specifically whenever he met a friend of mine.

His story went like this: In his early teens Edward helped at his dad's private practice on Harley Street. One morning he opened a drawer in the reception area and chanced on a bright yellow packet of holiday snaps. Eagerly opening them he saw indiscreet, suggestive photographs of Tracey, his father's receptionist, in varying stages of undress. When Edward, shocked and hurt, confronted his father, his dad shrugged. 'So now you know the truth. I'm a dog, a real dog.'

Edward later surmised that rather than secreting them away, he'd deliberately left them in easy reach. Years later his father walked out on his mother for another woman, the usual younger, blonder and thinner model, and to add insult to injury he had tried to get out of paying alimony to his ex-wife, Edward and his brain damaged brother who would need professional on-going care. It was like he wanted to cut them out of his life, his memory, and reality. How his conscience allowed him to do this I cannot understand. The left-behind family were devastated. Edward had developed an immune disorder that caused him unpleasant health upsets, perhaps exacerbated by taking on the paternal responsibility for his mother and elder brother, who lived part-time with his mother and the rest of the time in a care-home in the nearby Sussex countryside.

Edward's father was not a decent man and I felt for them all, but I did not like him bringing out his sob story so frequently for public airing. That he repeated it almost verbatim irked me. However, he always received the same response from listeners: high praise and approval.

'You are such a good man,' I heard on numerous occasions from friends and acquaintances.

We were seated round a drinks table at the Stanhope Arms in Kensington, near to where Louise worked as an estate agent. Edward excused himself from Louise and me. She had badgered me about meeting 'my new man'. I had known Louise since Heathfield and she was one of my more conservative and conventional friends with a lovely, warm heart and not great taste in men herself.

As soon as Edward's back rounded the corner, she leaned across. 'He is fantastic, Clea. I mean what a decent guy! He's really there for his poor mother and brother.' She trilled enthusiastically. 'You've got a real catch there.'

'I'm so glad you approve!' Louise head-nodded, revealing her part-Indian heritage to a tee.

'Well, Clea, compared to Alfie, come on! I mean, you know I did really like Alfie. He was handsome, interesting company and amusing, but he wasn't—' Louise took a moment, slamming her hand on the table dramatically. 'Responsible! He wasn't responsible, that's what it was. And selfish.' She was pleased with her deductions.

'You don't have to tell me. If I recall correctly, I was the one that went out with him.'

'Edward is a whole new ballpark. Dare I even say it?'

'Say what?'

'He's marriage material. Yes, that is what he is, really good marriage material.'

'Steady on. We've only been together six months.'

'Don't they say, "when you know, you know"?'

'We're still getting to know each other, but maybe. He's

keen on family, kids, all that. He adores his godson. I'm not convinced I'm the marrying kind. Well, okay, never say never, right.' I wanted this conversation to end.

Louise nudged me to let me know Edward was on his way back, loaded with drinks. Louise lowered her voice. 'You could always get pregnant.'

'You cannot be serious?'

Louise shrugged nonchalantly.

'What are you two girlies gossiping about, then?' Edward slopped his beer on the table, profusely apologising and Louise gave me a cheeky wink. I couldn't make out whether she was joking, or suggesting the most antiquated and manipulative way to seal the marriage deal with a man. Since my abortion at eighteen, I was always cautious regarding birth control, except for when I was addicted to crystal meth and self-preservation flew out the window.

Still, that Louise even jokingly suggested it made me think. Did I want to commit, and if so, was this the right man? I was in my mid-30s. Did I want children?

You know you are vaguely serious about a new relationship when you introduce a boyfriend to your oldest friends. But there were things my friends had no idea about, which I was grappling with in private. I was constantly overriding my emotions; he had a manner that suggested I should be grateful that he was with me. I still held in my innermost heart my dream of working as an actress, but the endless rejections had taken their toll. My self-esteem was lower than the ground floor and I had made the classic mistake of believing the frequent rejections represented my worth. I was fighting a constant battle with depression, which slunk in the background, always looking for its opportunity; I did not warn Edward about this for obvious reasons.

On the plus side, I was practicing as a Nichiren Buddhist and the philosophy was empowering; however, my delusion was deep and I convinced myself Edward was a result, a gift even, coming from my prayers, or rather chanting, an active form of meditation. It's a twice daily practice and I'd already felt the benefits in my mood and thinking, noticed a sway towards being more optimistic and hopeful. My decision to write a memoir about my addiction to crystal meth when I had lived in Los Angeles in my 20s had been a direct result of this practice and I'd committed to follow through.

As Plato acknowledged, all human behaviour flows from three main sources: desire, emotion and knowledge. They underpin pretty much everything in my experience. Throughout my life my tendency to become overwhelmed leads me into total self-delusion and lack of clarity. This manifested in all sorts of negative ways that lead me into self-abandonment, excessive drug use (in my 20s), low self-worth etc. My distorted perception made me behave in ways that I hated, but I seemed to have very little control over myself. They became repetitive negative patterns of behaviour.

In Nichiren Buddhism there is a concept called the 10 Worlds which addresses these states of life: we all switch between the lesser, middle and higher states of life—or worlds—throughout our day on a moment-to moment basis.

For example, my day might go like this: From waking up in a state of agitation to comfort as I stroke and feed my beautiful Maine-Coon cat Pickle, into momentary relief upon receiving some needed money into my bank account, to irritation with the neighbour leaving their rubbish too close to my car, to a sense of accomplishment having delivered a successful audition, to ecstasy upon receiving a phone call and being offered a great acting job. These states range from the very worse to the very best within me—Hell and Hunger, destructive despair and insatiable desires at one end to Buddhahood, absolute happiness, compassion for self and others, wholeness, a feeling of unity with the cosmos on the other end.

Chanting the mantra Nam Myoho Renge Kyo enabled me to become conscious of these different states, and perceive the most prevalent negative tendencies that were holding me back. By opening my eyes to my inner self, I could then start to transform myself; perform an inner transformation which is mirrored in my outer world. Chipping away on a daily basis at my karmic tendencies, some that run deep through both family lines, by the active-voice meditation of chanting. I also like to walk and chant, but that's just me.

This powerful spiritual practice is also known as the Mystic Law. Much of it is based on faith and belief, but I have experienced direct proof of practice. I could write a book on that. However, when it comes to my relationships with men, I am still very much a work-in-progress. In terms of Edward, my delusion was still paramount and my heart wanted what it wanted!

I knew I was resistant to questioning his suitability as a partner because a fellow Buddhist challenged me about him: this man recommended I chant honestly about whether this new man was right for my life. I had such a strong gut reaction to his heartfelt suggestion I dropped back from the regular meetings I usually attended, and my chanting became less consistent.

Part of me knew Edward was wrong, but I was signed up for the ride. And in a basic, almost child-like, dualistic way I believed I deserved a lucky break, and because it was not coming in my acting career it had to manifest in the love stakes.

Even though Edward outwardly despised his father he took pride in his many professional accomplishments. He'd had to choose between medicine and a career as a concert pianist. In fact, in a supreme effort to win over Heather, Edward's mother, he'd invited her out to a Rachmaninov concert. She arrived, took up her front row seat and could not understand where he'd gotten to when the ruby red curtain rose. She recognised his shoulder line, sat on the left side of the stage in front of a grand piano, now tensed and about to play as part of a semi-professional orchestra. She'd been bowled over by this dark, clever East End Jewish man with his mix of talents, and subsequently the piano had become a major part of Edward's life. He practiced every day on his upright piano in his living room, as part of his daily rituals that also included swimming copious lengths in the Olympic size pool at the Queen Mother Centre on Vauxhall Bridge Road, near to his mansion block flat. It always felt to me like he was daily physically punishing himself, following his drinking binges the night before.

Near Christmas, an old friend, Miranda from Heathfield, who lived in Notting Hill, invited us to her festive party, and again Edward impressed everyone with his tinkling of the ivories, although he missed a few notes due to drunkenness. My good friend Adam, a talented actor, met Edward for the first time and I knew from the get-go there was an uncomfortable undercurrent, which I put down to class rivalry, Adam being stalwart working class from Tottenham. The more drunk Edward became the more toffee-nosed he sounded, a common occurrence with Sloaney types, but I could see how jarring Adam found his comments. It was past midnight, our group was gathered in the bespoke kitchen, smoking and drinking.

'Isn't little Clea so pretty?' Edward took a couple wonky steps back to admire me, which struck me as verging on humiliating. I felt like a gelding being walked round the stable yard to be surveyed by the lord of the manor. To be fair he sometimes played out this patriarchal role with me, addressing me as Little Pretty, but he'd never done it in company. I cringed while I caught Adam's sniggering eye, who leaned in and whispered, 'You've got a live one there!' Not a good move on Adam's part.

'What's that you said, Adam?'

'Nothing to concern you, Edward mate.'

'Are you taking the piss out of me?' Edward advanced and squared up to Adam's wiry frame.

'Behave, Edward. Look, we really should go.' Having quickly lost focus, Edward was more interested in pouring the remains of a bottle of red wine into his empty glass.

'Steady on, old chap.' Adam was now properly taking the piss and I was uneasy.

'Hey-hey guys, we've all had a lot to drink so let's keep it nice, stay calm and carry on, okay.' I gave Adam a sharp look and he shook his head while raising his eyes. I felt judged.

'So tell me Adam, been working much recently?' I

nudged Adam as discreetly as I could.

'Yes, actually I just finished filming an episode for *The Bill*.'

'Everyone's done *The Bill*, haven't they?'

'Except me.' I weakly respond, shrugging. 'Not sure if that's a good or a bad sign really.'

'Well—let's face facts, Pretty, if you were going to make it as an actress you would have by now.' Adam's jaw almost dropped. 'At least you have your writing talents to fall back on.'

'Yes, well… I need to finish writing something first. Let alone make any money.'

'It's a tale of woe, your crystal meth story, Clea. It'll work out, don't worry,' said Adam.

'It's these poor sods who've spent decades trying to make it as actors that get nowhere. They're the ones I feel sorry for. They get to forty and what have they got to show for it.'

'What exactly do you do, Edward? Anything useful?' Adam interjected.

Before I could say Jack-the-Knife, Edward dismounted a sword from the wall and went into *en guard*, as if to fight a duel. Adam almost collapsed with laughter while I looked around for our hostess, hoping she had not seen our little scene and more importantly the nails Edward crudely knocked out of her wall where the decorative sword was crossed against its double.

'Like I said, you got a live wire there, Clea. You might be needing the fire brigade.' Adam mimed a gunshot to the head, which I chose to ignore.

'Edward! We are going now.' I grabbed him by the shoulders and frogmarched him to the door, hoping to find a taxi that would agree to take us. I was mortified by how he acted with Adam; I would need to bring this up.

On the street I noticed a minicab, a better bet than a black taxi. A couple weeks ago his bad attitude got us thrown out of a taxi and we had ended up walking home. To be fair it was both of us arguing about something inconsequential, but whereas I had backed down he insisted on yelling his head off and refused to stop when the London cabbie ordered him to pipe down. When he grabbed one of the pull-down seats attached to the partition and banged it up and down the cabbie lost his cool, pulled over and threw us out near Cleopatra's needle, along the Embankment. I left him stumbling on his own and hot-footed it to my flat, fed up, adamant I would end the relationship. I didn't hear from him for four days! Again, he gained the upper hand when he said, 'I was thinking of going to Sussex for the weekend. It's about time you met my mother and brother.'

I decided I would bring up the awkward end to the evening at my friend's party while we were sat in his shiny silver BMW driving down to Sussex.

'It was kind of a shame how things ended at Miranda's house the other night.' I used my most calm tone, giving him my coy sideways glance.

No response. Eyes straight ahead.

'Did you like Adam? My actor friend.' I tried another tact.

'Not really.' He shrugged, adding: 'Oh he was alright I s'pose.'

'Talking of drama that was quite a showy number you pulled yourself.'

His cold blue eyes stared at the congested road. Again,

no response.

'Don't you remember? You pulled one of Miranda's antique swords off the wall as if you were planning to duel Adam. It was very classical drama—maybe you missed your calling and it should be you playing the classical hero.'

He smoothly changed gear and accelerated up the hill, taking one of the many shortcuts to avoid rush-hour traffic.

'Can't remember a thing. Well, no one was hurt, were they, so what's the problem?'

His hand went to the stereo where he turned up Coldplay's 'In My Place'.

The morning after the night before, Edward was vaguely remorseful but did not suffer the avalanches of shame that inhabited me when I got drunk and behaved badly. Or maybe he was just thick skinned and refused, at this early stage in our relationship, to reveal his vulnerabilities. He never outwardly apologised, which unsettlingly reminded me of my mother.

In my experience, narcissists are incapable of taking responsibility, and although Edward was probably not one of those, he was certainly not keen on change or growth. This would prove the true sticking point between us. 'In vino veritas,' he'd exclaim, with his customary tongue click, as if that excused and explained everything. I'd learned early that post mortems were not to his liking and he'd rather disappear to the pool where he'd do an extra hour of lengths to assuage what I assumed was guilt. He could have just wanted to get away from me. I have no way to know.

We spent more time together than apart as we both had flexible schedules. I was writing what would become my first book, and signing on (to Edward's surprise; he'd never known of anyone who had done this) and he was supposedly making headway within the Tory Party ranks. But as I mentioned, nothing was what it seemed from the onset.

The best part about our relationship was the sex. I am loathe to mention this but it is relevant as to how and why we ended up together for three years.

Right before I met Edward, I saw a massage therapist in Brighton recommended by a new Buddhist friend. Near the end of the session the burly but sensitive Dave asked me if I had problems with orgasm. I was surprised, after all, he had been working primarily on my back, but he went on to explain he was sensing blockages around my ovaries and sex organs. 'And perhaps unresolved trauma to do with unwanted pregnancy?' I almost rolled off the massage table.

I sat up and swung my legs round to the side of the bed, ready to divulge what had happened and how I had ended up like this, amazed and excited he had chanced on something I found so difficult to discuss. He looked at me kindly and spoke in his low, deep tone.

'I'd rather continue with this body work on you, rather than enter into a dialogue about the narrative of what happened. Not to say it wouldn't be fascinating—' Dave gave me a glimpse of a smile, 'but I work better this way.'

I nodded.

He then told me to roll over onto my back and did this healing, unblocking ritual with burning scented oils, loud claps over my uterus alongside the sounds and vibrations of Tibetan singing bowls. I felt something dissipate—stuck energy?—and I left a whole lot lighter, with a fresh spring in my step.

A knock-on effect of this 'unblocking' was a revived interest in sex. With Alfie, sex had become so troublesome I stopped thinking about my pleasure: I was always trying to help him feel better. When I met Edward and the sexual side worked well, I felt relieved that there was nothing wrong with me.

Edward's punch to the right of my left eye threw me off balance and my right leg smashed into the sharp edge of the bleached wood coffee table. I toppled in a half fall onto the sofa. We had both been drinking. I'd made a point of not drinking that evening because I was to attend my writing workshop at the City Lit the next day, and had a critique planned for the manuscript I was working on. I'd diligently chosen a hefty section and prepared copies for my classmates, handing them out the week before. I was excited to hear what they had to say. Not that I was brimming with confidence, the opposite really, but the community and mutual support was encouraging and I enjoyed the class. It helped me feel not such a failure in the career stakes and gave me the encouragement I craved to continue writing.

Edward prided himself on his cooking. He had taught himself with the Delia Smith cookbook and he was sniffy about my efforts in the kitchen. I was happy to let him get on with it when we were together, although I felt he had hardly given me a chance; he'd been taken aback when I'd invited him to my dad's birthday dinner and all the food had come from M&S.

That evening he'd made grilled skate and a sort of ratatouille concoction to go with it. I didn't much like the skate and I went rummaging on his spice rack to jazz it up.

'Sorry I am not an artiste, like you Clea.'

'But you are. This looks divine.'

'Why are you adding that to it then.' He indicated the chilli powder and oregano.

'You know I like strong flavours.'

'So you say. But how come you're with me then. I'm a vanilla kind of guy, aren't I?'

'That's a weird way to describe yourself! I never called you that. We're all different, aren't we?'

'I'm just worried I can't live up to your exacting standards, Clea. All these crazy unconventional men you've known…'

I looked at him in disbelief. He was throwing back in my face what he'd read in my manuscript. It had taken me months to get up the courage to share it with him and he was using it against me. 'You know that was ten years ago and it didn't exactly end well, now did it?'

'I just don't see what you could find interesting in me.' He was fishing.

I yawned. Big mistake.

'Oh, am I boring you, I'm so sorry! Shall I go and put my slippers on now?'

'I'm just tired. It can be quite emotional; you know writing all this stuff down. First, I must go back and remember it all, no easy feat, and then get it into some coherent order.'

'Isn't that what writers do.' His arrogant tone irked.

'You know very well I haven't done much writing for a

while. It's like a muscle, it needs exercising.'

'You make such a big thing about everything, Clea.'

'I don't think that's true.'

'I bet that's just like your crazy mother, isn't it?' There was no question he was goading. I went in the kitchen to make myself a vodka and orange, a drink I don't like but I wanted something and that's all there was after he had finished the wine. My tiredness added to my muddy thinking and his last comment caught me off guard.

'Let's not bring my mother into the equation. It won't help anything.' I aimed to pacify and join him by the open French doors leading out to his balcony. He leaned on the door frame and was lugging on a cigarette like his life depended on it. The night air was chilly and the dark sky struck me as foreboding.

'Have I done something to upset you?'

'Why do you say that? Why does it have to always be about you?'

I shook my head wearily. 'I'm going to bed. I'm reading a good book.'

He didn't say anything and gave me what I could only describe as a mean look.

'That takes the biscuit. How long have we been together and already a book wins over time with me?'

'We do spend an awful lot of time together.' As soon as the misplaced word was out, I regretted it.

'Awful, eh? Well, if it's so bloody awful why don't you just piss off?' His face reddened.

'What I mean is neither of us is going out to a regular 9-5 job. We're really in a rather unique position, don't you think? We spend more time together than most couples can.'

I noticed his glazed eyes, but that the pupils remained alert in a subdued inner frenzy. 'Something needs to change, Clea.'

'What were you thinking about?' I asked tentatively assuming he was referring to his drinking, that I was fast joining him in.

'I think I need to leave the city.'

I wasn't expecting that. 'And go where?'

'Where do you bloody think? Sussex of course.'

'What about the Conservative Party and all that entails?' I hadn't mentioned that since I'd known him, he'd never done a day's work in their campaign office. We'd attended fundraisers and that was all. It was like his steam had run out.

Years earlier, he'd worked in the City as a metal trader, but decided—with his mother's help—that he wanted to enter politics. His mother, Heather, owned and ran successful Care Homes for adults with special needs. Knowing his straightforward and decent mother well, I knew she'd be mortified to know how Edward really spent his time: getting over hangovers by self-punishing exercise regimes, or spending time with me. Edward had not inherited her work ethic.

'Why are you bringing that up? It's nothing to do with you. You're a fucking useless distraction.'

'Thanks very much. You're hardly the greatest catch yourself.'

'I should have known to avoid you. Women with crazy mothers always turn out to be crazy bitches themselves.' Considering he had never met my mother, and categorically wouldn't, the rebuke incensed me. No doubt that was his intention. Against my better instincts I rose to his bait. A slanging match ensued, with both of us hurling our lost dreams and hopes at each other.

'No wonder your father doesn't want anything to do with you. You're a hopeless drunk.'

This remark landed his fist in my face.

I don't make it to my writing workshop. I don't make it out of my flat all day. I have a colourful bruise covering my right eye that is painful and swollen. I call the City Lit giving an excuse. I feel defeated with no idea on how to proceed.

The pervading confusion and humiliation are overwhelming. As if I had done something very wrong, even when rationally, I knew I hadn't. Having an argument with your boyfriend should not end up with a black eye. But he was drunk, I tell myself. Of course, drunken people do stupid, horrible things. I have done them myself, after all. But even I know violence is inexcusable.

Edward texts around lunchtime and I ignore him. He then calls three times and I decide to leave it a couple days, let him sweat it out. He leaves two plaintive and apologetic messages. I could report him to the police and he must know that. I convince myself that as this was the first time, it would also be the last.

Perhaps this was the shock Edward needed to wake him up? The push to address his alcoholism?

Time crawls as I lick my wounds, applying Arnica and part metallic bandage strips to reduce swelling. I creep into my local chemist on Wilton Road, silk scarf around my head with dark glasses. The Pakistani pharmacist is as helpful as ever and she suggests bandages. I tell her I'd tripped on my stairs and had gone flying into the banister. She doesn't believe me.

I feel stirrings of fury within, but dampen them; who can I speak to anyway? I am unwilling to share this 'secret' with friends because I know their advice will be straightforward: leave him. Instead, I buy an assorted bag of chocolate bars, and resign myself to stuffing my face and my feelings while watching TV. I have always been an expert at numbing out.

I ponder my situation with Edward. How well it had seemed taking time to get to know each other properly. But there was always this threat in the background that couldn't, wouldn't, stay there: his drinking. There is no doubt he had a Jekyll and Hyde personality. Sometimes under the influence he became silly and annoying, but more often he turned belligerent and unkind.

I feel deep down this is a cover for his unresolved feelings towards his father and unhappiness about the state of his life. I enact the co-dependent role to his alcoholic, believing it lies in my power to fix him. I am not ready to call it quits.

I recall the good times. A beautiful concert at the Barbican followed by a romantic dinner overlooking the Thames on Valentines night, a week skiing in Meribel, theatre trips, a week on the Cornwall coast, weekends in Venice and Dublin. Lovely experiences only marred when too much alcohol had been drunk by one, or both, of us. And at times it was me who verbally attacked him, finding reasons to criticise him, unfairly I know.

That aggression had been modelled by my mother and part of me needed love to receive attention, however negative. I will only understand this years after we break up, through therapy.

I investigate Love Addicts Anonymous, a self-help group to support people like me recover from misguided beliefs, conditioning and behaviours. This is the group's checklist to see whether one qualifies as a Love Addict:

Love Addicts Anonymous (LAA):

40 Questions to help you determine if you are a Love Addict. (Donated by Susan Peabody.)

If you can answer yes to more than a few of the following questions, you are probably a love addict. Remember love addiction comes in many forms, so even if you don't answer yes to all questions you may still be a love addict.

1.You are very needy when it comes to relationships.
2.You fall in love very easily and too quickly.
3.When you fall in love, you can't stop fantasising—even to do important things. You can't help yourself.
4.Sometimes, when you are lonely and looking for companionship, you lower your standards and settle for less than you want or deserve.
5.When you are in a relationship, you tend to smother your partner.
6.More than once, you have gotten involved with someone who is unable to commit—hoping he or she will change.
7.Once you have bonded with someone, you can't let go.
8.When you are attracted to someone, you will ignore all the warning signs that this person is not good for you.
9.Initial attraction is more important to you than

anything else when it comes to falling in love and choosing a partner. Falling in love over time does not appeal to you and is not an option.

10.When you are in love, you trust people who are not trustworthy. The rest of the time you have a hard time trusting people.

11.When a relationship ends, you feel your life is over and more than once you have thought about suicide because of a failed relationship.

12.You take on more than your share of responsibility for the survival of a relationship.

13.Love and relationships are the only things that interest you.

14.In some of your relationships you were the only one in love.

15.You are overwhelmed with loneliness when you are not in love or in a relationship.

16.You cannot stand being alone. You do not enjoy your own company.

17.More than once, you have gotten involved with the wrong person to avoid being lonely.

18.You are terrified of never finding someone to love.

19.You feel inadequate if you are not in a relationship.

20.You cannot say no when you are in love or if your partner threatens to leave you.

21.You try very hard to be who your partner wants you to be. You will do anything to please him or her—even abandon yourself (sacrifice what you want, need and value).

22.When you are in love, you only see what you want to see. You distort reality to quell anxiety and feed your fantasies.

23. You have a high tolerance for suffering in relationships. You are willing to suffer neglect, depression, loneliness, dishonesty—even abuse—to avoid the pain of separation anxiety (what you feel when you are not with someone you have bonded with).

24. More than once, you have carried a torch for someone and it was agonising.

25. You love romance. You have had more than one romantic interest at a time even when it involved dishonesty.

26. You have stayed with an abusive person.

27. Fantasies about someone you love, even if he or she is unavailable, are more important to you than meeting someone who is available.

28. You are terrified of being abandoned. Even the slightest rejection feels like abandonment and it makes you feel horrible.

29. You chase after people who have rejected you and try desperately to change their minds.

30. When you are in love, you are overly possessive and jealous.

31. More than once, you have neglected family or friends because of your relationship.

32. You have no impulse control when you are in love.

33. You feel an overwhelming need to check up on someone you are in love with.

34. More than once, you have spied on someone you are in love with.

35. You pursue someone you are in love with even if he or she is with another person.

36. If you are part of a love triangle (three people), you believe all is fair in love and war. You do not walk away.

37.Love is the most important thing in the world to you.

38.Even if you are not in a relationship, you still fantasise about love all the time—either someone you once loved or the perfect person who is going to come into your life someday.

39.As far back as you can remember, you have been preoccupied with love and romantic fantasies.

40.You feel powerless when you fall in love—as if you are in a trance or under a spell. You lose your ability to make wise choices.

Today I do not recognise myself in any of these traits and behaviours, and isn't 'love'—in all its myriad forms—the point of being alive? But most of it applied to me at some point or other… Hey-ho, life's a journey, not a destination.

Chapter 15

Glutton for Punishment

The happiness of your life depends on the qualities of your thoughts.

Marcus Aurelius, Meditations

After a week, I agreed to meet Edward at his flat. He sheepishly opened his door. We stood there apprehensively and awkwardly.

'Come here,' he eventually mouthed and I walked into his arms. He held me hard and sobbed into my shoulder. 'I'm so sorry, I'm so sorry. I promise it will never happen again.'

There was no mistaking his remorse. I asked about his drinking and how he was going to tackle that, to which he said he would give it up. I made suggestions that he see a counsellor and try Alcoholics Anonymous. He claimed he would be fine on his own.

I believed him because I wanted to. I also knew nothing would change, but this didn't stop me from hoping. The situation reminded me of how I always seemed to go on hoping things might change with my mother. They never did, not really.

'Why didn't you tell me this last night?' I search the living room for Edward's cigarettes, spot them and grab the pack.

'I thought there were more important matters on the table to discuss.' He is calm and reasonable, towelling his hair fresh from the shower.

'Where the hell's your lighter?' I demand. I had woken with unease. Maybe the break-up/make-up sex had been too familiar, too easy a reconciliation. My face is still painful and I feel like everything is slipping out of my grasp. Edward comes across to where I sit on the arm of the sofa and lights my cigarette.

'Thanks. So when did you cook up this plan to move into your mother's flat in Hastings?'

'To be honest—'

'A bloody good place to start!'

'Don't, Clea. I mean, look, come on, be reasonable, hear me out.'

'I think I am being very reasonable, considering!' I turn my bruised face full on to where he stands across the room, leaning on his mantelpiece. The sun from the French windows makes me squint; Edward quickly looks away.

'My mother and I have been discussing this for a while. Me going into her business with her, taking more of an active role. It makes sense. Actually, it's essential I go live down there.'

'I just can't believe you never mentioned it to me until it's a *fait accompli*. I thought I was your girlfriend for fuck's sake.' I grab another cigarette and light up.

'You're chain smoking.'

'You're one to talk. I really don't need you on my case right now.'

'Touché… So how about this? Come down with me tomorrow to Hastings and we can decorate the flat together, buy furniture, have a look round. And of course, it's a great place to get lots of writing done.' He gathers me in his arms again as I accidentally drop ash on his carpet. 'I do really love you, you know?' he whispers.

The flat had a beautiful sea view. The balcony was big enough for a couple chairs and a small table and there were already terracotta pots that looked lovely planted with flowers, a project I chose for myself. The small, modern block was new and pleasant in a boxy, neat way. His mother bought two flats in the building as investments.

We'd finished supper when Edward returned to the wardrobe he was putting together. We had spent half the day at IKEA where our tastes clashed miserably. I had traipsed behind him wearing the largest sunglasses and woolly scarf to hide residual bruising. The general busyness of the staff and the unrelenting hordes allowed me to feel less paranoid about how I looked.

Ed was all functionality and plainness, whereas I favoured character and style. He always won in the final draw because he was paying, and it was his flat. As much as he proclaimed we were sharing a life, the reality was different.

'You'll need to be out all day tomorrow, Clea.' Edward's voice was drowned by the washing up so I yelled to him to repeat himself.

'What? Why?' I stomped over where he sat amidst flat pack furniture.

'I told you my mother was going to be coming round

at some point.'

'And?'—He pointed at my face, shook his head and went back to tightening screws into bleached wood.

It felt like a blow to the stomach. But it made sense. 'Of course. What would your mother think if she saw me like this?' The swelling had gone down but the bruising was blackish blue and speckled green. It was obvious. It was also what could only be described as clenched fist shape with knuckle marks; 'walking into a door' wouldn't cut it.

'I think it's going to take at least a month to heal, if I'm lucky. Thank god I don't have any auditions coming up.'

Edward looked up from his DIY. 'I'm really sorry, but I can't put her off.' I harrumphed off for an evening walk along the front, thinking that he could put her off if he really wanted, but his relationship with her was more important to him than his relationship with me.

The next morning Edward woke me with tea and toast. He then hurried me out the door and, in my haste, I forgot my makeup bag. I hadn't been able to face myself in the mirror that early in the morning so I'd planned to stop by a coffee shop, drink a strong coffee and then apply makeup, or rather paint foundation over my bruises in their toilets. Walking quickly, I left the narrow walkway anxiously looking out for his mother's car, feeling like a filthy rat scurrying away, out of sight and in shame. I stopped by Boots in town to check their concealers and bought mascara; two young, female sales assistants pointed at me, turned to each other, and whispered. I tried to ignore them, quickly buying my things and exiting, humiliated by the sting of stigma.

Dejected, I walked along the windy front and sat on

the pier, enjoying the skittish baby seagulls. I chanted to myself looking out at the big, wide sea, looking, and hoping for answers. We'd made up so why did I feel so bad? What was I missing? Where was I going so wrong?

Over coffee an hour later I noticed that the film *Mona Lisa* was on at a local cinema, a short bus journey. I have used cinema as a therapeutic means of identification, cathartic release, enjoyment, and escape since I was a child. For me it functioned similarly to how others used silent meditation. In the dark and cold cinema that afternoon my heart was breaking knowing that there was a lie playing out, but I felt powerless to break its spell, and this was mirrored in the scene near the end of the film when Julia Roberts' love interest is revealed as a fraud. I was screaming inside.

The irony that struck me the most was that Edward's best friend Jago had come for dinner a few weeks ago and asked me to become the Agony Aunt for a website he ran. He offered to pay a set amount per reply and I was excited to take him up. So here I was advising other women about their feckless boyfriends, yet my own relationship was a mess. I was a total fraud.

One of the best parts of my relationship with Edward was the relationship I had developed with his mother, Heather. She also confided in me when we spent weekends at her house where she kept up a stunning garden with glorious herbaceous borders, roses, smart green lawns and heaps of organic home-grown vegetables. We sat at the large kitchen table over a cup of tea.

'I really am glad Edward met you, Clea.'

'I'm glad I met him too.'

'You know I was becoming quite worried about him.'

'Really? In what way?'

She took a sip of her tea and looked into the middle distance. 'Let's see. Well, he seemed so directionless. And for rather a long time now.'

'But he seems better now?'

'Oh yes, definitely.' I smiled at her, wondering how she had got it so wrong too, although I liked her insinuation about my influence.

'He always had these girlfriends who were nice enough, but didn't seem to have much substance. One was very glamorous. Liked to walk around with very few clothes on.'

'The dark-haired model. Oh yes, I heard about her.' I don't mention how devastated Edward was when she aborted their foetus; he claimed he was more upset about it than she was.

'I thought she was rather grasping. Something untrustworthy about her; she's the type I could see living as a high calibre you-know-what—'

'Prostitute?' I laughed. Heather was very conservative and I doubted she had ever met one. I had been careful to reveal little to her about my life in LA. She'd likely question my suitability for her darling boy. After all, he was number one.

'Yes, I've heard about all his exes.' Heather gently rolled her eyes at me; although Edward was her *raison d'etre*, her opinion of men was low. I did not repeat Edward's prideful account of how he'd had sex with three different girls on the same day when he was travelling in Australia on his year off.

When we'd met I'd found the tales of his exes amusing

and somehow validating of his virility and attractiveness to women; clearly I did not authentically trust my own instincts. Maybe I intuited something was off, but I couldn't recognise it then.

'Have you been in touch with your mother, Clea?' I shook my head, grimacing unconvincingly. It always hurt my heart when my mother was brought up.

'It's such a shame. She's the one really missing out. You're a wonderful person and I really enjoy spending time with you. Now let's see—shall we get lunch together for our hungry boys? I was thinking we could eat outside as it's such a lovely, sunny day.'

'Absolutely. I'll lay the table out there.'

I think Heather was a major draw in keeping me in the relationship with Edward. I felt safe and happy whenever we went to stay with her; she was a stable, caring and decent mother figure. She'd always show immense interest in everything I was involved with—my new role as an Agony Aunt, Buddhism, acting, my writing—something I had never experienced before.

I knew if I stayed with Edward, I would have a replacement mother, if I didn't cross her or her boys.

Edward's non-drinking lasted eight days. We were at his mother's preparing a BBQ on a Saturday night. He was stoking the coals with a beer in hand, looking like he had not a care in the world.

I double took when I clocked him lifting the beer bottle to his mouth, and he gave me a 'that's life' shrug combined with a half-smile that didn't hold an iota of an apology. My heart fell and all I could do was take myself to our bedroom to chant. I was too upset to act fine.

I returned half an hour later feeling slightly calmer, positive we could move forward. Jago and his wife Kiri had arrived with their son Freddy who was nearly two and already fast asleep. Edward loved to BBQ and was in his element. Heather had a few friends there as well who she worked with. It was a beautiful summer evening and I looked around at the bright, luscious garden peopled with happy faces and thought: Okay, everything is not exactly perfect, but it is good enough.

I had pushed into the depths of my mind the physical violence, and was living on a prayer that it was a once off. That happens, doesn't it? A momentary lapse of reason, exacerbated by alcohol and circumstances.

I liked Jago, Edward's best friend, who had a sensitive and kind nature. He'd been bullied at Harrow and Ed had always done his best to protect him.

According to Jago, Ed became a Rottweiler under provocation, which I had initially found hard to believe. He had met his wife when he and Ed were travelling in Australia. It had been a love at first sight situation with him and Kiri, who was part Māori. She was a practical and sensible type with a thickset body and beautiful rich brown hair that went past her bottom, clearly her best feature. Jago was cute, gangly, tall and already losing his hair.

Edward had claimed Jago married Kiri, the first girl he had properly kissed, because he was terrified no one else would ever like him enough again. I could see, however, that they fit perfectly and even enjoyed the same quiet hobbies like playing cards and fishing.

Edward, Kiri and Jago chatted amiably over the embers of the fire but I managed to grab Jago's ear, away from everybody else. I suggested we walk to the furthest fence where the neighbours' horses, including a chestnut foal, would be grazing, knowing he was an animal lover.

'Oh yeah, by the way Clea, hits are way up on the site. Well done.'

'Brilliant! That's me, Agony Aunt Extraordinaire.'

'Well, I was going to get rid of that site, but now I won't. And someone called from that daytime TV show *Kilroy* to see if you'd be interested in being on it, part of the panel. I thought that would be a great idea, especially if you wear a t shirt with the website emblazoned over it.'

'Are you kidding me?'

'No, I'm not. The producer wants you to call her after the weekend, I'll give you her number before we leave.'

'I seriously doubt they'll allow me to wear a shirt with urdumped.com scrawled on it. Before you go and get a whole load made up.'

'Really? That's a shame. It would have been great advertising.' I almost gaped at Jago's naivety. I quickly looked over my shoulder to check Ed's whereabouts; he was still chatting with Kiri, probably entertaining her with bad jokes she would be too polite not to laugh at. I noticed him swigging from a fresh beer, back on autopilot.

'Look Jago, there's something else I wanted to talk about.'

'Really? What?'

'Oh god, don't look over at him; he'll know we're talking about him!'

'I was wondering about him, to be honest. I'd hoped he'd maybe changed but—'

'So you know about his drinking?'

His look said, 'no shit Sherlock' while I let out a long sigh.

'It's probably got worse, right?'

'I wouldn't know, but I'd say that's standard. But you tell me? When did you first notice it?'

'Years ago, Clea. I was very worried about him. I moved in with him in Victoria about five years ago now, only for six months while Kiri was sorting her visa so she could move over here. Well, he was getting really pissed every other night. And he wasn't working. He was supposed to be involved with the Conservatives, but I didn't see evidence of real commitment in that direction. I tried to talk to him but drew a blank. A total blank!'

'Been there.'

'Eventually I called up an alcohol helpline. I explained my concerns, but they told me there was nothing I could do, as his friend, unless Ed wanted to help himself.'

'That's pretty standard advice. But there's something else too—'

Jago turned to me, with a kindly look of concern on his friendly, beaky features.

'What? You can tell me. I'd like you to feel you can trust me, Clea.'

And then I held back what I wanted to share with him because it felt like the utmost betrayal to Ed who was now pointedly looking over at us both. I couldn't, even though I desperately wanted sensible input into how to progress with Ed. Watching him organise the BBQ, delegate duties, eat, drink and chat like everything was normal struck me as wrong. Like a form of cynical denial and debasement, but who was debasing who?

'Oh… I'm worried about him working with his mum.

I mean it's hardly stimulating or interesting work, is it?'

'I wouldn't worry about that. If anything, the regular schedule should help, enforce discipline. Heather's fair, but strict too. She grounded Ed for a month on his summer hols when we were sixteen when she caught him smoking.'

I laughed, thinking what a merry dance we were all leading. 'He still pretends he doesn't smoke. When he's here he sneaks off to the barn.' We both shook our heads and exchanged a shrug. Denial was the order of the day.

Later that evening when a drunken Ed climbed into bed next to me, I pretended to be asleep. He snuggled up and spooned me, placing his arms around my waist. I was struck how I wanted to move out of his hold, but didn't. The discomfort of his proximity was easier to override than a late-night conversation. I wanted to yell at him, 'A week, just one week and you are back on the booze', but I contained my fury, something I was practiced at doing.

'Is that Clea Myers? This is Sergeant Wilson, I'm in charge of your complaint. Is now a good time to speak?' I pick up having slept late, sleeping off the hangover and horrors of the night before.

'I suppose,' I mumble. A long pause follows.

'We'll be needing you to come down the station.'

'Why? I mean I haven't got anything else to say… about it.'

'These are very serious allegations. You will have to come into Paddington Green. It's straightforward procedure.' His tone is firm, no-nonsense.

'Doesn't seem that straightforward to me.' I mumble irritably.

Why won't they just leave me alone? The inevitability of the situation makes me shudder; I am nauseous and beaten, physically, emotionally and spiritually. Here I am a year later in the same position with a smashed-up face, just worse this time.

The fighting is more out-of-control, the damage to my face worse. There is no way I am going anywhere until the swelling on my right cheek goes down.

'When can you come down the station? How about tomorrow then?'

I want to scream at this insensitive moron to leave me alone, but I can't find the energy, or inclination. Also, something about his calm tone and slow, rhythmic cadence lets me know he is on my side. I had gone some way to overcoming my hatred towards the police since I was arrested and brutalised in a psychotic episode under the influence of crystal meth in the mid-90s. I had even permitted an undercover drug unit to use my living room as a lookout on a drugs bust on the Lillington Gardens estate I lived on in Pimlico. They left a right mess behind, which struck me as somewhat rude. If you're using a civilian's flat as a 'look-out' at least clear up after your crisps and fag butts.

'Where's Paddington Green then?'

'It's right by Edgware Road.'

'That's quite far.'

'Have you been in contact with the man that attacked you?'

'You mean my boyfriend?'

'Edward Dunsmore. I suggest you have no more contact with him.'

'Right.'

I go back upstairs to the darkness of my bedroom where I climb under my duvet. Choked sobs emit from my heavy heart, but it hurts too much to cry.

The evening started well. I met Ed at his flat where I left my laptop, which had been playing up. Ed had always been good with computers. We took a bus into the west end to attend a screening of a short film I was in, based on a Shakespearean Sonnet, at the Soho Curzon on Shaftesbury Avenue. I was looking casually smart in a pink silk pencil skirt with a belted loose black shirt, with black leather boots; my '*Sex in the City*' garb, Ed called it. He'd never seen me acting before so I was equally excited and anxious. We were on an even keel for a while. He was living down in Hastings and I would visit regularly, while he'd also kept his flat in London as he wasn't ready to cut all ties.

Secretly I hoped he would change his mind about living and working in Hastings after a year or so; it struck me as a limited life; most of our arguments there were over the TV guide. He'd joked about us getting married and how the guests would be people who worked at the Home.

I had weakly laughed, but felt depressed by the insularity of our coupledom. Besides Jago and his wife, Ed's social circle had diminished and my own wasn't great, to the point that a couple of my good friends had commented how insular I had become. The lights had gone down after the director said a few words and we watched the film. It was a well-made short with good performances, nicely shot and edited.

I had no idea what Ed was expecting but when it

finished after twelve minutes, and the clapping had faded, he looked around and announced, 'Is that it?'

'Shhhh! That's what shorts are like,' I whispered in his ear and grabbed his arm and nudged him out of the screening room to the bar.

To my surprise, Nate was standing in the corner of the bar chatting with a round-faced, plump man in a pale blue suit. I hadn't seen him in over three years, but the last time we spoke on the phone, about a year ago, he'd told me about his upcoming nuptials to a producer on one of his shows. They'd held it at Kenwood House and I had been slightly hurt he had not invited me.

When I joked about my invitation getting lost in the post, he'd rejoined, 'You have to be absolutely mad if you think Linda would let you anywhere near me. She's most definitely the jealous type.'

I could hear the edge of pride in his voice; he was chuffed to have found a partner who felt this strongly about him. I had been genuinely happy to hear his news. I waved at him and he gestured for me to come over. Ed was sorting drinks for us and ingratiating himself with the film's director. He liked to make a decent impression with new people.

'How's married life treating you then, Nate?' I made a point of sounding genuine.

'You know what, Clea, it's really great.'

'Glad to hear it.' The man in blue was briefly introduced, another comedian, Duncan.

'Don't forget to tell her the good news!' Duncan said, poking Nate in his ribs in a vaguely camp gesture. Nate looked away, slightly embarrassed.

'Go on!' Duncan clinked his glass against Nate's in a

way that I knew what was coming next.

'And we're having a baby,' Nate announced sheepishly.

'Wow! I'm really happy for you both, I really am.' Ed had sauntered over with our drinks and I introduced him to Nate and Duncan. I sensed he wasn't too comfortable by what I privately thought of as his trying-too-hard demeanour.

'Really loved that late-night show you were on Nate. Always caught it when I was pissed after the pub on Friday nights, although I would have watched anything.' I looked at Ed, inwardly cringing. 'And that girl, whatshername, she's a bit of alright, isn't she?'

'I went to drama school with her. She's actually gay,' Duncan added.

'Give us her number then. We can have a threesome, can't we, Clea.' I tacitly ignored him.

'Nate's just told us his wife and him are expecting a baby.' Ed reached across to clink Nate's beer glass.

'First sprog, is it?' Nate nodded, and then looked pointedly at me.

'Clea, I'm compering for a mate at the Amused Moose just over the road on Greek Street if you fancy coming. Starts at 9pm. I can put your names on the door if you'd like?' I was relieved at the quick change of subject.

'Okay. Great! See you later then.' Duncan had already moved off to talk to someone else he knew, and Nate threw his man-bag over his shoulder. I was struck by how cool and trendy Nate looked in his designer haircut, cargo pants, trainers and Superdry anorak compared to Ed's black jeans, brogues and blazer. As if he'd read my mind, Nate leaned in and whispered, 'See you've reverted to type.'

'What was that? What did he say to you? I bet he was being rude about me.' Ed oozed petulance.

'Not everything's about you, you know darling? He just said "nice to see you".'

'Hmm, I bet. Thought he was bloody married.' Ed harrumphed off to refill his drink, while I debated whether seeing more of Nate in one evening was a good, or bad thing.

'So now I get to see the great Nate in all his glory!' Ed was chucking back the booze and taking the piss out of me. We'd moved to The Coach and Horses with Joe, one of the actors from the short film with whom I'd always gotten along. Ed had been talking himself down, saying what a boring life he had compared to me and my glamorous acting world. Both Joe and I had nearly collapsed laughing at that. But Ed was ridiculously convinced, as well as steadily drunker and Joe soon made a quick getaway like he could sniff something unwholesome in the air.

We stumbled along Old Compton Street towards the venue where we arrived late and stood like sardines leaning against the high bar. It was all females on the bill besides Nate; I found them all funny in their own way. Ed seemed more interested in drinking. At some point he went off to the loos and when he returned, he had a strange, unreadable expression.

I had run into an actress girlfriend I'd not seen for months so we were having an exuberant catch up between acts. Mandy was a mouthy Eastender with bright orange hair. When Ed returned to our table, having stopped at the bar to refill his glass yet again, she nudged me jokily.

'So this is the new man is it? Where've you been 'iding Clea away then, eh?'

'I can assure you Clea does exactly as she pleases.'

Mandy raised an eyebrow at me.

'I'm Ed. And you are?' he asked stuffily, extending his arm like an army general. Introductions were made, but I could see Ed was bored.

I made our excuses and we left. In the taxi back to his flat, he announced he hated all us 'lovey' types. I decided to keep quiet. If I hadn't left my laptop at his flat, I wouldn't have gone back with him because there was a strange undercurrent. I felt oddly restless and suggested he had a look at my laptop but when I saw him fumbling with it, I figured he was probably making it worse so suggested we watch a DVD instead.

'How about I mix us a Caipirinha?'

'What now? It's getting a bit late, isn't it?'

'What's the problem, Clea? I am up here on a jolly, after all.'

'I thought you were here for that Conference tomorrow, as well as my screening.'

'It's not school you know. I don't get a black mark if I'm late.'

'I never said that, now did I? I just thought that maybe, just maybe, you'd want to get there early. You know, what with it all being new and stuff.'

'Oh, whatever. I'm only going to keep my mother happy. It will be deadly dull.'

'I'm sure it might be, but on the other hand it may surprise you.' He gave me a sharp look.

'Like Nate did, you mean?'

'What are you talking about? Nate's lovely, don't you

think?'

'I imagine there are parts of him you found particularly lovely? His dick, perhaps?' He gave me a lopsided, drunken wink while I tried to understand.

'Are you talking about his penis? What, where?'

'Didn't I mention I ran into Nate in the Men's at the club? Yes, all was revealed and I definitely feel very much the lesser man.'

His drunken childishness hit a nerve. He'd been making digs at me all night and I was fed up.

'Well, maybe you bloody well are the lesser man.'

I quickly looked away as I said it.

Big mistake: As his fist swung from below and upwards, landing on my left cheek, I was flung across the room.

His anger was palpable and for the first time I was genuinely scared; like something wild had been released.

I stumbled and fell against the wooden frame of the French windows. Clearly unable to look at me, Ed went into the bathroom, locking the door quickly behind him.

I grabbed my laptop off the table, my sixth sense telling me he might smash it out of spite. I stumbled along the road trying to shove the laptop into the bag while grappling inside for my mobile phone. Once I found it, I pressed 999.

'I just left the police station. It was really heavy going.' I raised my voice to Ed over the mobile while I turned off Edgware Road into a quieter side street. Sirens blared in the background echoing how edgy and jolted I felt.

'Well, what did they say?' Silence. He repeated himself and I could hear the barely masked fear in his voice.

'Right, well.' I took a deep breath. 'They say I should press assault charges against you. That I owe it to other beaten women. All that sort of thing. They were pretty decent.'

'Right. You know that my new career will be destroyed if that happens. I work in the care field and—'

'Look Ed, I know that. I don't want to ruin anything for you, but—'

'But what?' His voice was on the verge of tears and reminded me of a couple months ago when he'd got drunk and destroyed a large electric heater in a rage, smashing chunks of white plastic with a replica sword that sat on his mantelpiece. I watched in amazement and then had the neighbours to contend with who were not best pleased, banging on the front door and threatening to call the police. I could hardly ignore what had become a running theme, could I?

'Well, I know you're sorry, but this time, that's not enough.' I could hear sobs now. I felt bad for him, I did, as he seemed so child-like and pitiful. But a quick glance at my reflection in a shop window snapped me back to reality. The swelling had gone down, but the bruising was an ugly tapestry across my cheek.

'Well… what… then?' Ed sniffled.

'Anger Management for starters. And then there's the drinking.'

A long pause.

'I'll have to call you back. My mother's just pulled up. We've got a meeting.'

That told me where his priorities lay, if I hadn't already worked it out. My Buddhist practice was helping me get back on track; my confidence was shattered. Even though

Ed claimed he loved me, what kind of 'love' was he offering? I'd have moments of clarity when I'd imagine he was out of my life and felt an incredible surge of freedom, but then I'd think back to the loving moments between us and it would get muddy again. Like the Lotus flower, I knew I would blossom again, out of this muddy pond, but would I take Ed with me, or leave him behind in the murky depths?

Between his promises and tears, I could not forget 'the incident' that now had a police case number. My love had gone. There was a part of me that felt he should pay for what he'd done, but even with the police behind me it seemed better to move on, without a fuss. I understand the police's point of view regarding domestic violence, but I knew I had a history of violence in past relationships, which made me reconsider. To be fair, Ed had never had this happen before me; I know he could have been lying about that, but it rang true.

The relationship ended over a brief phone call in which we agreed it was over. We were a match destined for hell. Afterwards, I cried at the loss of Heather.

I heard through Jago a year later that Ed had married a woman nine months after we broke up.

I acknowledged Ed's support to me in *Tweaking the Dream,* in the print book, and he emailed to congratulate me after it came out.

Chapter 16

Ithaka gave you the marvellous journey.
Without her you would not have set out.
She has nothing left to give you now.

C. P. Cavafy, Ithaka

Alone

The period following my break up with Edward, I chose to follow my innate seeking spirit. I could see a disturbing pattern of mistakes, and realised something significant needed to transform within me. That's not to say I swore off boys completely, but they took a backseat.

I stopped drinking—I needed a mental, physical, and emotional detox, and became more involved with the Nichiren Buddhists in Pimlico, where I was now living.

I'd made steps repairing my relationship with my mother. I had evolved, and she had mellowed with age. I had been out to stay with her and my stepfather in France and naturally the subject of me and men had arisen.

'Why can't you just meet someone normal,' opined my mother. Backed by her husband: 'Yes, someone we can enjoy meeting. And hey kiddo, maybe a couple of sprogs too?' He'd always wink at that, like he didn't believe it would happen.

After the first days of my visit things grew more fractious and I'd spent more time chanting to calm myself and transform what had been habitually angry responses resulting in combustion between me and mum. Considering where we'd been, these behavioural shifts were miraculous and I believed a result of my Buddhist practice; my mother even acknowledged this and spoke respectfully of my Buddhism, although she also thought it juju.

Part of me was still desperate for their approval, but I also chanced upon some knowledge that deeply resonated. A parent has the power to be a scaffolding to help their child build themselves, or a cage to imprison them. The difference? Do you allow your daughter to surpass you, or see their growth as a ladder to boost yourself?

I was treated like a structure for my mother to climb. My life was always hijacked by her. I understand she was starved of growth and meaning and feel compassion for her, but I also acknowledge my anger at being used and allow myself to grieve. Not only the lack of a loving parental relationship, but the pain of being unable to connect with my true self, impact my choices, and prevented me from living an authentic life for so long. This ended; I refused to be another lost, lonely soul wandering the earth draining and devouring others, and using my pain as an excuse.

There was another visit to France that holds fond memories for me. A gay, English couple who were good friends with my mother and stepfather had an Alpaca farm in San Sulpice, a charming village near Mansle in the Le Charente area. They needed a house-sitter for their Alpacas, dogs and chickens when they went away to

Barbados for a month. My mother mentioned this to me on the telephone and to her surprise, I jumped at the chance.

That trip was my most successful ever in regards to my relationship with mum. She would drive over every day from Mansle, and we would drink tea, chat, take a walk, open the little farm-shop that sold items made from Alpaca wool, and laugh over not much at all. Little and often worked for us, and it was just that month. One Sunday I drove to theirs' for a traditional English Roast and mum said, 'If only we could do this regularly like a normal family.'

If only.

I had brought my Gohonzon, my Buddhist scroll, with me and she joined in with me a couple times chanting for ten minutes. The fact her favourite pop star Tina Turner was also a practitioner helped! Mum's favourite Alpaca, Marvin, was dark and temperamental; we'd walk by the field and he'd come running to her for pieces of apple. She'd joke that she preferred Marvin to her husband. Of course, there were sticky moments between us, but looking back I think perhaps she wanted to heal something too.

Self-love is the love I needed to restore within myself. It starts from the core and emanates out. I was learning to love myself by honouring my needs. I'm focusing on my need to act, play, write and express myself fully. I'm entitled to that, it's essential to my being.

I need to remind myself I'm entitled to my needs, wants and desires. They may not be fulfilled, but I'm allowed them. That was a lesson that took me more than half a lifetime to learn, but I have learned it well.

Chapter 17

Charles: Final Nail

The road of excess leads to the palace of wisdom.

William Blake, *Proverbs of Hell*

Charles had started messaging me through Facebook, around when my first book was coming out in 2009.

Like many writers I'd received numerous rejections, but I'd refused to give up. My gut drove my belief that my story needed to be told, that it might do some good in the world. 'Transforming poison into medicine', as the Buddhist belief goes. I'd become a spokeswoman for FRANK, the drugs awareness charity, and shared and spoken eloquently on numerous TV and radio news shows about the dangers of crystal meth gaining a foothold in the UK. The drug was also classified as 'B', which I knew would send the wrong message to users; primarily, that it was relatively harmless. When my agent refused to look at smaller publishing houses, I embraced the recent POD (print on demand) route.

I knew all forms of publicity and marketing would be up to me. I was feeling strong in myself when Charles started to 'poke' me on Facebook, making vague, saucy overtures. With a book to promote I was open to rekindling old friendships and making new ones, within the auspices of networking. I gave him my mobile number; it was as if Charles could read my mind.

'Why have you been avoiding me? I don't bite you know.'

Hilarious. I responded with the usual claptrap about being busy; he continued in his upper-crusty articulated tones playing his winning hand: 'You do know who my family are, don't you?'

'No, I don't. Should I?'

An exaggerated sigh followed, suggestive of 'silly me'.

'Well, my dear, we happen to be huge in publishing—books, magazines, you name it. The reason I mention this little fact is that I see you have written a book. A rather interesting book.' I clocked the compliment.

'Yes. Yes, I have. Why?'

'Well. Maybe I can help you? Stuff that, I know I can.'

'Are we talking about world domination?' I jested. I felt slightly wrong-footed.

'My dear Clea, that is exactly why I am calling.' He proceeded to name drop magazine editors, and a newspaper publisher. Already I envisioned fabulous reviews and write-ups in the nation's newspapers and magazines, ones that would not usually review, or deign to notice, a POD book by an unknown author.

Looking back, what I find strange about this dalliance, for that is what it was, is that I did not clock his alcoholism. I was not drinking, and he had that clever alcoholic habit of masking.

Denial is powerful! I can only surmise I liked him, and if I saw the truth I would need to back off. I'd had my fill of addicts and alcoholics, so I believed. Like all of us he had good points. Initially, when he was winding me in, he was charm personified, but the shift proved glaringly ugly.

Providing some explanation as to my state of mind, it was around this time my health declined dramatically. Age 37, I had extreme mood swings, hideous aches, and pains in my joints—mainly in my hips and legs—with intermittent periods of exhaustion, alongside hot sweaty flushes out of nowhere that eradicated any traces of makeup, bar panda eyes, in minutes.

Blood tests showed my ovaries had stopped working. After months of medical exams, I was diagnosed with Premature Ovarian Failure; I was unequivocally devastated that I had no more eggs.

I have often heard it said we never know how lucky we are, until our luck runs out! I had not given nearly enough thought to motherhood; indeed, I'd assumed it would happen for me, just later, say on the cusp of forty.

I also felt bereft, as if my womanhood, alongside my femininity, had been ripped asunder. I was being treated at Chelsea and Westminster hospital and the best option presented was hormone replacement therapy (HRT). Did I mention all this made me feel much older than I was, and I perceived the HRT as essential. In truth, I wish I'd allowed my body to balance itself; however, I felt it had abandoned me, let me down.

I was never going to have babies, or even a baby.

This affected me profoundly. I resented my body, I blew up to size 16, due to the synthetic hormones and emotional eating, and was unhappy. It seemed to appear with no warning.

I recalled I'd had a secret crush on Charles at fifteen. He

was dark-haired then, before the grey set in, with a rather aristocratic look—wiry, whippet-faced with a slightly hooked, elegant nose. His deep-set green eyes suggested wisdom.

A school-friend from Heathfield, part of our peer group, openly lusted after him so I never mentioned my crush to anyone. We all abided by the unwritten girl code. Charles was a persistent flirt and egotist. An icky incident beckons to the front of my mind. We were a gang of five sat round a table in the basement of *Pucci's Pizza* on Kings Road, late one evening. Our teenage evenings always started in a pub, either the Shuckburgh Arms, The Admiral Cod or The Australian, followed by pizza and Sambuca shots before hitting the sticky dance-floor of the 151 Club, five minutes' walk up the road, that ultimate 80s Sloane disco. I loved the deep red décor and winey smelling basement. By my early 20s I had moved on to what I perceived as more sophisticated and hip establishments, but always held a soft spot for this place.

Charles sat across the table from me in *Pucci's*, smoking, a slow grin spread across his face. 'Hey Clea, have you ever thought of investing in Clearasil?'

'What do you mean?' Within a millisecond I knew exactly what he was referring to, and felt my spotty face go beetroot.

'You know! Why not buy shares in the company as you need so much of it: Clearasil Clea.'

I had no comeback. No experience of dealing with bombastic teenage boys. From twelve to twenty-five I had acne. Not the worst type, leaving skin scarred and pitted for life, but bad enough I was self-conscious and had quickly become what I thought was a great applier of makeup, mixing and blending cover-up and foundation as if my life depended on it. Bizarrely, my skin cleared when I regularly used crystal meth, although I would not recommend it.

That Charles could make such a mean joke at my expense says a lot about him, but what teenage girl isn't sensitive about her appearance. I am, at times, overly sensitive, so perhaps it was not meant to be mean, just a jibe?

When Charles and I first meet for coffee, I mention the Clearasil incident, but he has no recollection of it. He dangles his connections before me and we arrange to meet again for lunch. I give him eight copies of my book.

Charles turns the book over and double-takes. 'Holy shit! That's you?'

'One and the same.'

He looks down and up at me a few times dramatically. 'Nooo way!'

'Well at least I made it down to a size zero.'

He glances at me blankly, clueless about what I am referring to. Some things only women and gay men understand.

'I was very skinny with drug-induced anorexia,' I explain.

For our second meeting, I bundle the lunch date with a hospital appointment. It says something about where my head is at that I am meeting a man from my way-back past—on a date pretending to be a business meeting—ahead of another dreaded trip to Chelsea and Westminster hospital to sort out my hormonal problems. I remember shaving my armpit in the shower that morning and edging the blade in too sharply, while pinky-red water streamed onto white tiles. Surely a bad omen?

I have not entirely lost my desire to please men, as I wear a flowery strapless summer dress of a light, flowing fabric that makes me somewhat flat-chested. Charles jokily comments on this after his third pint at the Builders Arms.

I suggest a walk around Chelsea, and we end up in St. Luke's Gardens on Sidney Street. Within moments of entering the gardens, Charles finds a secluded bench under a weepy willow. He regales me about his first and second marriages and divorces, between lighting cigarettes.

I learn that he met his last ex-wife in a night-club, as a randy teen, when she'd been visiting London from Australia. He'd then reconnected with her through Facebook. They'd fallen in love in cyberspace, and for real when she'd visited him in London. He overshares about their sexual exploits in taxis and other places. I smile politely, and look at the time.

I sense he needs to talk, and who am I to stop him? I am a good listener, and take this as a positive character trait. It's also an essential skill as a performer.

I clock how Charles loves his own voice. It feels like being held hostage, but I smile and nod in the appropriate places. This feeling is not uncommon for me during this time: it is like my character and personality is subsumed by the hormone imbalances and subsequent chronic fatigue. My voice lapses, choked within me. I become extremely passive.

In my core, I have little to offer anyone. I will know later that this is just another symptom of chronic fatigue, but it never sits well as it is against my nature to be chronically depressed.

I accept people that need to open-up about their journeys, since I have been on a personal mission of self-improvement since my mid-20s—one that embraced numerous groups and belief systems including the Temple of Thelema, Christianity, Christian Science, Reiki, Guru Mai, the Twelve-step self-help programs like Narcotics Anonymous, plus numerous visits to Tarot card readers and psychic mediums.

Charles details how things between him and his ex-wife took a darker note once they moved from the suburbs of Brisbane to a farm in the outback. To my ears, it sounds idyllic.

'I really miss Ned and Kelly!' Charles wipes a tear.

'So, you had kids?' I query.

'Kids? Oh no. God no! Ned and Kelly are my Australian Ridgebacks. Dogs!'

'Where are they then?'

'Still on the farm, as far as I know with her.'

I also believe anyone who loves animals can't possibly be a bad sort.

A long pause follows.

'That's when the violence started.' His tone softens while he glares ahead. I notice he has also gone slightly pink in the face, I assume out of embarrassment, or shame.

'Violence?' I query, alert. Something inside me feels queasy.

'Yes.' He lights another cigarette.

'I know a little something about that.' I offer.

He faces me, an unknowable, distant look in his eyes. I

instinctively edge away.

'No! It's not what you are thinking,' he proffers.

I don't know how to respond.

'That is when she started to attack me.'

A long silence ensues. Oh dear, I haven't signed up for this. I check the time and comment that I will need to press on to the hospital soon.

'Stay a few minutes longer, please.'

'What happened?'

'*Radio 4* had a whole program about it last week. I called in!'

'Sorry, you've lost me. You called in about what exactly?'

'Female violence against men.' He sounds slightly smug. Again, I get an uncomfortable sensation in the pit of my stomach. Does he know Alfie? Of course, he doesn't.

'She attacked you, did she?' I act surprised.

'Damn right she did. I was a house-husband for a while, not my fault, you know—sorting out my work permit—and all that. Actually, I quite liked it, you know—gardening, cooking. Well, then I went and got a new job as a head-hunter and I had to visit clients all over Oz. Loads of flying.'

'Sounds fun.'

'Yes. That was part of the problem. Of course, I missed her, but it was all rather fun. Very social, lots of beer and golf. Horse racing too, some cricket thrown in for good measure.'

'Bit of a never-ending jolly by the sounds of it,' I joke, to lighten the tone.

'Every time I came home, she'd pick me up from the

airport. Then she'd attack me in the car.'

'When she was driving?'

He looks perplexed. 'No. I drove us back. But when you are driving and a mad woman is attacking you, there is very little you can do about it.'

'I guess not.' He seems lost in his world now and I feel awkward.

'I need a drink.'

I leave him at a pub nearby, while I race down Fulham Road to the hospital.

Charles proceeded to love-bomb me. Endless texts and late-night calls. The promotion of my book gave him ample opportunity to yank my chain. We met often, over months. I'd always suggest a café, but soon we'd be back in a pub, the domain he seemed most comfortable in.

'Aren't you a clever girl then? Who'd have known.'

'Did you think me stupid?'

'Well, I don't remember thinking you were brainy.'

'Because I'm not! I'm decidedly average.'

'Well, it takes some brains to write a book,' he insisted.

He gave me the lop-sided smile I remembered from twenty years ago. He did charm well, but what I really wanted to hear was how he could get me press coverage through his fabulous, high-flyer contacts. Initially, he'd been so adamant he could create a bestseller!

Charles swilled the dregs of his pint and grinned. 'That's better. I felt pretty rough today.' He winked at me.

'Heavy night, was it?' I queried innocently.

'You could say! Yes, I guess we could say I am now off the market.'

His tone was decidedly jubilant.

I felt flattened. 'Who's the lucky lady?'

'Let me get another drink and I'll spill.'

And women are called the gossipy sex!

Charles had now been validated in my eyes, by the fact another woman wanted him. I'd felt there was something off, but my green-eyed monster took over. He'd regaled me with the story of how they'd hooked up, through an old friend in advertising. Amanda and him hit it off immediately; they also shared the same birthday. She was a divorced single mother of a teenager and had a big house in Henley-on-Thames. She'd been invited over the previous evening to share a takeaway, but no food was eaten. Her hunger was for him, so Charles claimed.

I didn't hear from him for days after and felt that was best. I assumed he was having a grand time getting 'his tail away' (his words). But late one evening my mobile rang.

'Who'd ever have thought a nice English girl like you could get into so much trouble. You little rebel, you!' His gravelly voice almost-whispered into my ear. His excitement was palpable.

'Does that mean you like it then?'

'Yeah sure. It's a good read, made better by the fact I know you. I don't really get all the addiction stuff, but it's very interesting.'

I sensed his denial, but it wasn't my job to fix him.

He was in an off-on relationship with Amanda, that sounded like he had the better deal.

Again, he was very keen to have 'business' meetings with me. He was vague about his work commitments. He made a big thing about how busy he was, but managed to spend a fair amount of time communicating with me about everything, anything, and nothing.

Lengthy telephone calls late at night became commonplace, even when he was staying at Amanda's house. It was very flirty. In preparation for another lunchtime meeting he sent this message:

'High Noon—Cab rank at Victoria. I'm the guy with the look that says: "Come and make me smile and yet we must be serious for a moment as we have a book to sell." xx'

And another time:

'Oh boy, you really are something, just not quite sure what… X'

And then higher terms of endearments were suddenly in use:

Darling Clea,

In response to your last missive: I'll tell you what I am Clea. When I'm on a mission, I will not lay down, I will not sleep until the mission is done and we achieve our goal. Sad but true. I will sell your book—not because it's a good read but because you asked me to. Perhaps not the case at weekends dear, but see you at 12 tomorrow. Xx

Messages pinged between us and the sexual tension mounted, although occasionally he dropped in a comment about Amanda. I should have called him on it, but didn't. I also never heard anything more about all his great contacts. He was good at the chat, but not action.

However, we'd quickly established that we were on the same wavelength. I fell for him.

Things reached a vaguely steamier level when we were

sat outside a pub on Tachbrook Street in Pimlico. He'd had a few pints already, whereas I was on the diet Coke.

He grabbed my hand and shoved it under the outdoor picnic table, onto his erection, straining against his black jeans. I could feel myself going beetroot.

'Looks like I am going to have to pole vault home!' He laughed.

I was at a loss. The blurred lines between us were too smudged for comfort. So I fabricated an excuse and raced away. I wasn't handling the situation well, and knew it. My libido was almost non-existent following the issues with my ovaries, and even though I was needy for male attention, I was not in touch with my own sexuality.

Charles' obtuseness unsettled me.

He moved in with Amanda in Henley, but was still calling me. He had laid off with the sexual innuendo, to my relief. We'd had marathon phone sessions sharing our innermost thoughts and feelings. Like one does at the start of a romantic relationship.

One night he described the moon over the river to me. It was past midnight and he'd gone out to smoke by the Thames. I assume to be out of Amanda's range of hearing.

For the first time, I'd shared with him my hope that this highly recommended acupuncturist in Kensal Rise could resolve and fix my infertility.

'I cannot think of anything better in the whole world, than having a baby with you. That would just be incredible,' Charles whispered into the mouthpiece.

Heady stuff.

Heady, but also strange: discombobulating. Why was he talking about having a baby with me when we hadn't even had sex yet, and he was living with his new girlfriend? Throw into the mix my over-reliance on this Chinese acupuncturist who swore she could restore my fertility—she could not—and I was a mess. I wasn't going to be bearing anyone's children and certainly not Charles'.

With hindsight I can see he was doing that manipulative thing whereby he revealed supposed secrets about himself with the game-plan of dominance.

It worked for a while. And then it did not. We met up one last time.

I made the mistake of drinking. The white wine hit hard. I lost my temper because he was continually sending me mixed messages, literally and figuratively. Amanda was still around, yet he was proclaiming love for me.

A glass was broken—I threw it at the wall, next to where he sat—and shards splintered everywhere; I still have a tiny scar on my forehead.

The next day, the last I heard from him, he emailed me the song, 'Fix You' by Coldplay.

Six months later, I was still smarting over the whole sad experience. I heard through a mutual acquaintance that Charles had gone into rehab in Thailand, for his alcoholism.

Soon after I chanced on a Facebook post showing him on the steps of Chelsea Town Hall, having just got married to a tall, striking black woman. Both wore huge grins while she batted away confetti. I clicked through on the name tag of the woman—naturally my curiosity was piqued—and realised he'd married one of his counsellors.

I wished her luck.

EPILOGUE

I am not afraid of storms, for I am learning how to sail my ship.

Louisa May Alcott, Little Women

Anything you can imagine you can make real.

Jules Verne, Around the World in Eighty Days

When I started writing this book, ten years ago, the little girl inside secretly hoped for a 'happily ever after' ending. I did get the Happy Ever After, but not the conventional one sold to me when I was growing up.

I thought I had been done with all the difficult internal work upon the release of *Tweaking the Dream*, but I discovered I was only beginning. And how amazing is that?

I learned more about Intergenerational Trauma, Complex-PTSD alongside Narcissistic Personality Disorder, and how all these affect a child to the core: I stopped believing there was something inherently wrong with me. I realised I was not hideous, ugly inside and out, unfixable, undesirable, stupid, a loser or any of the other insults and criticisms aimed at me throughout my life, from my life-giver, my mum.

I feel it's only fair to say my mother was not to blame

either. She was just repeating the inherited patterns of abuse, body-shaming, violence and humiliation that were meted out to her by her own mother. Who knows how many generations back it goes? I first clocked something was off with the Grannie/Mum dynamic when we visited her at her last independent home in Brighton, before the OAP home in Hove took over. She'd been hospitalised and we went to pick her up and move her into a council bungalow on the Whitehawk estate; any money had been well and truly spent, at this point, bar a meagre US pension. Grannie had broken her wrist, but that didn't stop her getting hold of a bottle of gin as soon as we stopped at the shops.

An hour later and the vitriolic diatribe at her daughter was quite something to witness. It was so toxic it felt like I was watching a scene from a play, but I think that was how I disassociated from it. And we were there to help her; she had no friends left, in fact I never heard of her ever having a friend. But my grannie was always nice to me. When she'd had money again, after her second marriage to a rich Jewish-American from New Jersey, she'd delighted in spoiling me with cuddly toys from Harrods. She even bought her groceries there!

By the time she was carted off to the home her mind was addled by her steady diet of fags and booze. She entered that child-like state of wonderment and general sweetness, peppered with sporadic demands for biscuits and tea. She forgot that she was a smoker and drinker, and lived for another fourteen years. They were most fond of her at the home.

When I understood, in my bones, that my subconscious belief system that ran the show—my life—

had been programmed with faulty software, I experienced a new me. A rebirth. Now I had something tangible that made sense of the insanity I'd witnessed at home, with Mummy—her insatiable rages, suicide attempts, put-downs, rejections, and abandonment on too many occasions to recall—and I knew, in my soul, I was not to blame.

The woman had issues, sad ones, but also behaviours that meant she alienated most people. Melanie, her best friend, stuck around, but nice as she could be, I'd say her emotional intelligence was so low my mother's comments *et al.* did not faze or affect her.

This realisation set me free! When I spoke with Mum, I maintained stronger boundaries and placed more emotional distance between us. I'd telephone once a week and my visits to Le Charente-Poitou became fewer. My strategy backfired, in the end, but I did not feel responsible.

My stepfather received a lung cancer diagnosis and my mother was not supportive. He was her main support—he did everything to place her centre-stage—and now he needed her. I knew this was not going to end well.

Sadly, her cruelty manifested in the last year of his life when he was struggling through chemotherapy. He'd tolerated and waited on her for almost 40 years, and endured her insanity for decades, but she could not cope with his health needs taking centre stage. She railed against him and his 'fucking cancer', wailing: 'What about me, what about me?'

Before he died, my stepfather and I spoke for the last time, from his hospital bed. 'Mark my words, Clee, your mother won't last longer than six months without me. Our will is with Pierre, the notaire in Mansle.'

Mummy lasted almost seven months, but that was only because she'd been on suicide watch. She'd stopped me attending my stepfather's funeral because she was going to Portugal with friends immediately after, and I would have been an inconvenience.

I'd been in India for a couple months and I'd left answer-machine messages for her, but I could tell they had not been picked up. I had been in one of my favourite places in Goa, Palolem, thinking how much I wanted to bring Mum out here with me. Maybe we could repair our relationship now Johnny was gone? In our case, three had always been a crowd.

I'd just got home to London when Melanie called to let me know Mummy had died, by her own hand—an overdose. It was her third attempt in a month. She had to create a ruse, and hide in her barn because locals were checking on her, but she was nothing if not determined. She had always despised the idea of growing old, and now she was spared those indignities.

She had been held in a mental ward in a hospital, but persuaded the doctors she was fine. She also had made Melanie promise not to contact me about her failed suicide attempts, and subsequent stay in the hospital. It angered and mystified me that Melanie had not ignored her demand, but also meant it was a *fait accompli*, and I was spared more battles with my conscience.

As time had gone on, and I'd become more familiar with myself, or the core of who I am, I considered 'no contact' with my mother. That is often thought to be the best way to break free from an abusive narcissist. Instead, my father and I had offered her the chance to live with him in his Whitstable home. That might sound strange, but my father still cared about her and I was impressed by his generosity; he was almost 90. She claimed to think about it—her finances were a huge worry to her, although she had enough money to stay afloat—but declined.

I never knew she'd given away Carlo, her last black pug dog, before Christmas, right before I left for India. If I had known about Carlo, I would have understood her plans.

From what people who knew her told me at the funeral, which I arranged near Angouleme, she rarely mentioned me except to tell them, 'I was a useless drug addict.'

She did not leave a note.

I was left in shock. After I entered her house, and went into the barn and up the rickety stairs to see where her last moments had been—so many blisters of pills, how she got hold of them I have no idea—the notaire stopped by. He requested I come by his office later that day, which I did.

He told me that my mother had changed her will months ago: she had taken me out of it. In my place, she'd left what she had—not much in the grand scheme—to an English couple she'd befriended in her final years who'd been very attentive to her, as much as anyone could be.

To this day, I almost laugh at how she got the 'Last Word' from the grave.

In 2019, I was diagnosed with breast cancer. I had treatment for Grade 2/Stage 2, ER/PR positive breast cancer, the most common type; one in eight women over the age of 50 receive similar diagnoses.

I had turned 50 the week before and had been

celebrating what I perceived as the next 50 golden years to come; no more narcissistic mother on a mission to destroy me, and no more elderly father, or other elderly relatives to help support and look after.

I perceived it as a sort of breaking free. Breaking loose of the familial shackles that were my upbringing and social conditioning. I'd had some highly progressive and good years in therapy and was reaping the rewards. It might sound crazy, but the first thing my therapist had me do was work out what I liked and didn't. This covered everything from food, dog breeds, people, to hairstyles and clothes. I also had acting successes and felt good about myself. I was dating again.

The breast cancer diagnosis devastated me, initially. It felt unfair and wrong, producing a despair within me I hadn't experienced since my mother's death. I felt alone, abandoned by my diseased body again. There's no question the cancer was triggered by intense loss over a four-year period: my stepdad died of lung cancer, followed by my mother's suicide, and then my dad about three years later. Moreover, my beloved black and white cat got cancer, and had to be put down six months after my dad died. It felt like the final kick in the gut.

I am strong, but it was one hurt too many.

During cancer treatment I was alone, single, with no children, but I had the support of kind friends. I think I chose—subconsciously—to do the treatments by myself. If nothing else, my upbringing taught me self-reliance.

Cancer teaches you many things, but for me the main awakening was the innate healing power within my body, alongside an appreciation for the everyday: good friends, a beautiful sunny day, a walk in the park. The mundane became glorious and I appreciated being alive.

I needed to teach myself love: self-love.

I thought I was fixed and 'done' with 'Tweaking the Dream', but I discovered I was only beginning. And how amazing is that?

This experiment of tracing back through these relationships has empowered me in ways I could not have comprehended at the start.

Let's rid ourselves of shame. Let's become empowered with self-love and emanate outwards like a beacon call to peace and love. I hold my head high knowing I have written my truth, and through it claim back my empowerment within it.

Naturally I am sad that I will never bear a child and experience that specific form of motherhood, but I can nurture myself and others, and utilise that aspect of my nature in my relationships with friends, colleagues, random people I chat with on trains, planes and in coffee shops. This sadness and regret was not of my doing. It happened to me, not because of me, as I had been conditioned and taught to believe growing up. There is a place for my herb-infused, spicy personality and the greatest lesson I've learned is that we can only be dis-empowered by ourselves, and in turn by understanding that, we can only empower ourselves. It comes from within us, not from outside.

From revisiting these boys and my journey alongside them, I can see how lacking I was in these basic traits: self-respect and love.

Go online and a quick search will reveal thousands of tutorials and magazine articles about overcoming the narcissist in your life, and I'm glad that others can educate themselves quickly and at a younger age than myself.

Undeniably, the damage can be undone, I'm proof.

I still believe in romantic love. I would like to share my life with a partner. The difference today is that I don't need a partner to complete me.

I do that very well by myself.

Useful Resources:

Louise Hay, *You Can Heal Your Life*, Hay House, 1984
Susan Jeffers, *Feel the Fear and Do It Anyway*, Vermilion, 2007
Julia Cameron, *The Right to Write*, Macmillan, 1998
Natalie Goldberg, *Writing Down the Bones—Freeing the Writer Within*, Shambhala, 1986
Elizabeth Gilbert, *Big Magic*, Riverhead Books, 2015

www.talktofrank.com
www.mind.org.uk
https://slaauk.org/
https://hsperson.com/
https://highlysensitiverefuge.com/
https://uksobs.org/

Soka Gakkai International, (worldwide Buddhist organization based upon the teachings of Nichiren Daishonin):
www.sgi-uk.org
www.sgi-usa.org
www.nichirenlibrary.org
Richard Causton, *The Buddha in Daily Life*, Rider Books, 1995
Daisaku Ikeda, Lectures on *On Attaining Buddhahood in This Lifetime*, SGM, 2007